Y0-ELA-419

*Frontispiece*

# PRACTICAL BASKETRY

BY

ANNA A. GILL

TEACHER OF ORTHOGENIC CLASS, KENDERTON SCHOOL, PHILADELPHIA

DRAWINGS BY THE AUTHOR

PHILADELPHIA
DAVID McKAY, PUBLISHER
604-608 South Washington Square

COPYRIGHT, 1916, BY
DAVID McKAY

689

TO

THE MEMORY OF

MY FATHER

St. J.

106450

# CONTENTS

# Contents

# ILLUSTRATIONS

# Illustrations ix

# PREFACE

Basketry is one of the oldest and most valuable of the crafts. As far back as the time of the Israelites we read of its usefulness in offering sacrifices. Of necessity it was born, and in its infancy was made into simple forms, but very soon its importance to man was so duly felt and appreciated that new forms took shape, and its uses were so extended that the early basket makers vied with one another in producing pleasing work and in discovering new and various kinds of materials to put into it.

Though the Chinese and Japanese have sent us, for long years, marvelous things of beauty, it is to our American Indian that we owe our debt for beauty and artistry of this industry; for industry it is.

It seems quite impossible to me to write on basketry without mentioning the Indian and his connection with it, for we can very safely call him the master artist of basket work. In its history, and a romantic one it is, the Indian figures first and last. The Indian woman was never satisfied with the materials just at hand; she sought for and tried all kinds, in season and out of season, and she chose, unerringly, the best. Her patience was without limit in her experiments in materials, dyes and weaves, with the result that her basketry is the peer of any in the world. Her sample work was nature—and into every line of her basket she wove a meaning symbolical of something in particular.

Serious study of Indian basketry would serve both as an inspiration and stimulation to better work: its intricacy, its poetry and its artistry would be a revelation, and give a fuller understanding of a people so sadly misunderstood.

Basketry was used by the primitive Indians in carrying water. When there was a scarcity, and careful conservation was necessary, the basket was the article used as a conveyance. Some of the California Indians up to this day use their baskets successfully as cooking utensils, while the bassinet, made out of basketry, was, and is still, used by the Indian to hold the papoose.

Basketry is an important factor in the promotion of education. Its wide influence is felt not only in the class room but in homes, settlement work, blind institutions, asylums, in fact in institutions of all kinds. The importance and influence of basketry is being recognized now and the work is being carried on in earnest. Within the past five years it has made a great jump and in most institutions where manual training has been introduced, basket making has attained a prominent place in the training of the child.

Basket work is a valuable aid in the character building of the child, for, through it can be given lessons in patience, perseverance and concentration, while truth and honesty can be effectually impressed on the worker, resulting in the gradual though steady developing of the will power.

Our reorganized school systems show what a specific educational value manual training has, not alone in the manual skill which the child attains, but also in the mental, moral and economic values which it gains.

The desire to construct and create is strong in childhood, and here in basketry will be found an astonishing aid in inspiring such desire and in developing constructive ability. Children, especially boys, find it fascinating and it is a work which appeals to them in all their moods; frequently when they are unable to do any other kind of school work they turn with delight to basketry.

The child who works steadily over a basket, and may have it to weave and reweave many times before completing it satisfactorily, is not only receiving a valuable lesson in patience and thoroughness, and gaining much experience which will be of inestimable value later on in this particular work, but he is being trained into an efficient workman of the future.

Basket making, which handwork the children love best to do, not only develops their judgment, makes keen their observation, makes them discriminating, but it has a stimulating effect upon their minds and awakens in them the desire to put forth their best efforts. Hanging baskets, scrap baskets, trays, etc., mean something more to them than a piece of basket work done merely because of its utility. Instinctively they recognize the true intrinsic value of the work and that they are real workers, but also it is the beauty and the surprises in basketry development that has its strong and attractive appeal for them.

Owing to the simplicity of basketry the work is being generally accepted. The child of seven or eight years may make a simple mat and basket and find it play work, while the older child may make beautiful useful baskets and trays for the home.

Originality in the child has full play and should always be encouraged since the field of work in this ground is abundant; and he should never be discouraged, no matter how loose the weaving may be nor how crude it may look: he will soon be able, through comparison, to discover his mistakes and correct the poor work.

I would suggest that children be permitted to criticise their own and each other's work.

The celebrating of the holiday seasons can be nicely carried out in the manual training period when the making of birthday gifts, Christmas trays, Easter baskets, sewing baskets, hanging baskets and scrap baskets can be appropriately introduced. Try this suggestion, and watch the happiness of the child who makes gifts for his loved ones.

Sequence in basketry should be followed carefully with beginners, and although it will be impossible to give in detail all the steps included in the subject, the most essential and important will be given, with many suggestions in models for advanced workers.

In conclusion, just a word to the special class teacher of backward, defective, and the backward or defective delinquents. The course presented in this book may be used in the sequence given or adapted just as is necessary to the class of children taught.  Most of the models here demonstrated have been successfully taught to children in the backward delinquent class and have been a means of promoting, mentally and morally, the welfare of the child; directing his miscontrolled energy into proper channels, besides making his school life a brighter and happier one.

That this book may be of help to the basket maker and that it may bring much success and happiness to the reader is the wish of the author who has spent many happy hours in preparing it.

# EQUIPMENT

# PRACTICAL BASKETRY

## CHAPTER I

## EQUIPMENT

### MATERIALS

The materials used in making these baskets are rattan or reed, raffia, rush, straw, hemp.

Rattan is a palm which grows wild in India, Japan, China and East India Islands. The rattan seed is black and corresponds in size to a pea. It is a notable fact that, while growing, the rattan always faces the sun. The shoot of this seed grows four years; it is then cut close. The plant produces almost three hundred shoots which are cut annually. These slender shoots attain a length of from three to five hundred feet. They climb the highest trees and hang from them in graceful festoons. It is interesting to see how, like the selfish pumpkin vine, they crowd out any other plant that should happen to be in the way. By small fibres which spring from the joints, they fasten themselves to the trees, and they hold so tenaciously and have such grip or strength that it requires several men, sometimes as many as a half dozen, to separate and remove them.

The reed is manufactured from the rattan.    It has been manufactured in America for about sixty years.    There are a number of such manufacturing plants, among which the Wakefield Rattan Company and the New England Company have made splendid reed.    Germany and Belgium give us the best reed, while the least desirable quality comes from China.

The outer surface of the rattan is glazed.    It is cut in long narrow strips, and is familiar to everyone under the name "cane."    It is used in caning chairs.    From the pith or inside rattan, we get the reed known as oval, flat and round, the latter being most extensively used.

The round reed varies in sizes from No. oo to No. 17; No. oo being the finest, is used in making the centers of baskets, in finishing handles, and in making very small baskets and trays.    Sizes 1 to 5 are used in making ordinary size baskets and trays, 5 and 6 for scrap baskets, 8 and 10 for handle foundations.

The reed comes only in the natural color, but

may be dyed into many beautiful colors either before or after the article is made.

Oval or split reed comes in sizes 5 and 7. This reed makes artistic hanging baskets.

The flat ⅜ inch wide is often used in making foundations for sweet grass baskets, and it also makes durable scrap baskets.

Raffia is the outside covering of the Madagascar palm. It is a light, tough material imported in the natural or straw color, but may be dyed in many beautiful colors. It is sold in bundles or braids of from one to four pounds. Care should be exercised in using this material. It is advisable to keep it in canvas bags or hang it in braids in the class room, as careless handling may cause untidiness or tend to disorder in the class room.

Rush, flat or braided, is imported and sold in the natural and dull green colors. The flat rush is sold by the pound, the braided by bundles or bunches. The braided rush makes a strong scrap basket; it must be soaked before using to prevent cracking. The flat rush is used in making smaller baskets.

Straw is used as a weaver, and can be woven either wet or dry, but it is better to dip it in water a few minutes before using. Round and oval scrap baskets may be made by combining different colors of the straw with the natural color.

Hemp, which is imported from the Philippine Islands, may be used as a foundation for raffia and sweet grass baskets.

## Tools

Very few tools are necessary in basketry, although, to the basket maker, who intends doing much work the following articles are essential: pruning shears, awl, plier, galvanized tub and bucket, measuring stick or rule, knife for splicing the reed. Rubber fingers may be used. For the dyer, rubber gloves and large earthen pots are necessary.

# THE FIRST LESSON

## CHAPTER II
## THE FIRST LESSON

Reed is a brittle material, therefore it must be soaked in water before using. The time required depends on the number of the reed used. No. oo merely dipped in water can be used successfully. Nos. 1 and 2 can be used after soaking in water ten minutes; Nos. 4 and 5 after fifteen or twenty minutes. Either cold or hot water may be used, the hot water consuming less time to soak the reed than the cold.

No. 4 and No. 2 reeds are commonly used together in ordinary sized baskets. No. 4 for the spokes, which form the foundation upon and around which No. 2, as the weaver, is woven.

The weaving of a round mat or basket is begun in the center and woven out toward the end. It is absolutely necessary that beginners master the fundamental steps, for no basket can be well made that has a poor bottom. In order to avoid this, the mat is practised upon until the art of weaving a good center is accomplished.

The following are the commonest weaves used.

SIMPLE WEAVING is the commonest of all and is the continuation of under one spoke and over the next.

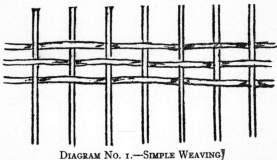

DIAGRAM NO. 1.—SIMPLE WEAVING

DOUBLE WEAVING, the same as simple weaving, only that two weavers are woven together as one.

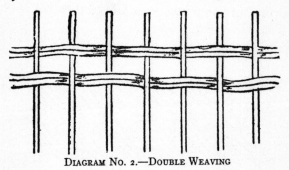

DIAGRAM NO. 2.—DOUBLE WEAVING

PAIRING.—Two weavers are inserted back of two successive spokes and crossed between, the

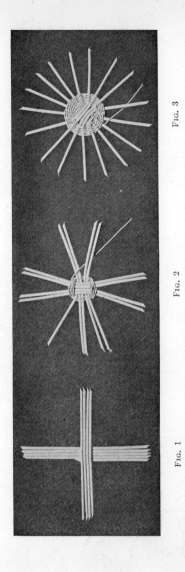

FIG. 1     FIG. 2     FIG. 3

under weave brought forward each time and made the upper weave. This may be used on an even as well as odd number of spokes.

DIAGRAM NO. 3.—PAIRING

DOUBLE PAIRING.—The weave is the same as pairing but two weavers are woven together as one.

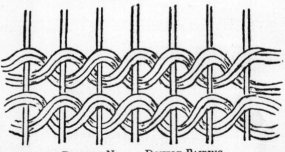

DIAGRAM NO. 4.—DOUBLE PAIRING

TWO AND ONE WEAVE.—Simply a weaver

woven in front of two spokes and back of one spoke. This makes a pretty effect in oval reed.

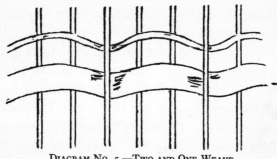

DIAGRAM No. 5.—TWO AND ONE WEAVE

THREE AND TWO WEAVE.—One weaver woven in front of three spokes and back of two. This weave is used with oval reed and rush, in making scrap baskets.

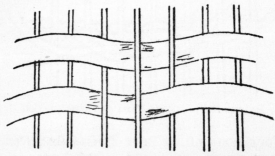

DIAGRAM No. 6.—THREE AND TWO WEAVE

TRIPLE TWIST OR THREE-ROD COIL, sometimes called the "Wale" Weave.—Three weavers start back of three consecutive spokes. Beginning with the first spoke to the left and weaving to the right bring the left-hand weaver out in front of the next two spokes, back of the next and out in front. The second and third weavers are treated in the same way, always bringing each weaver in front of 2 spokes and back of the next one. This weave is used mostly in beginning the sides of separate bottom baskets where the spokes are inserted, and in the ending of baskets. It is a strong foundation for borders and handles.

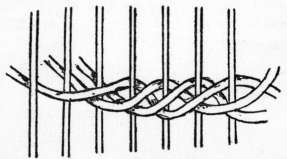

DIAGRAM NO. 7.—TRIPLE TWIST OR THREE-ROD COIL

FOUR-ROD COIL OR ROPE TWIST.—Is woven in a similar manner to the three coil weave except that the weavers are brought in front of 3 spokes and back of one.

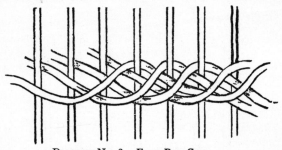

DIAGRAM NO. 8.—FOUR-ROD COIL

FIVE-ROD COIL.—The weavers are brought in front of 4 spokes and back of 1 spoke.

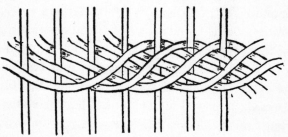

DIAGRAM NO. 9.—FIVE-ROD COIL

UPSETTING.—Simply a strong weave used in turning up a basket. Three rows of a three or four coil weave are usually used in making an up-setting on a scrap basket.

SLEWING.—Two or more weavers used as one in single weaving.

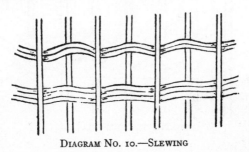

DIAGRAM NO. 10.—SLEWING

THE SIXTEEN-SPOKE CENTER means sixteen spokes arranged in groups of fours in the following manner: first, four spokes are placed in a vertical position, the next four in a horizontal position over the first four, the remaining eight spokes arranged in diagonal positions, one diagonal four laid over the other diagonal four in an opposite direction. A weaver is placed under the left-hand horizontal group and simple weaving is woven over one group and under another until four rows are completed. The spokes are then separated into groups of twos by bringing the weavers over and under every two spokes instead of four. This may be finished either in simple weaving with one weaver, or by inserting another weaver, in pairing.

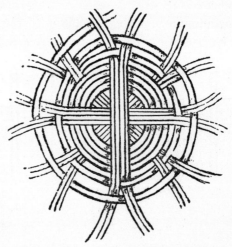

DIAGRAM No. 11.—SIXTEEN-SPOKE CENTER

In cutting the ends of spokes always cut obliquely to prevent the reed from splitting.

In splitting spokes, the incision must be made carefully in the center of the spoke. Do not make the incision larger than is necessary.

DIAGRAM No. 12.—A SPLIT SPOKE

Half of the number of spokes needed should be split in center, and the other half inserted through the incision.

In beginning a new weaver join it to the other weaver by crossing both ends back of a spoke.

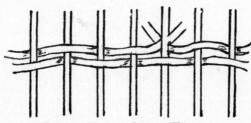

DIAGRAM NO. 13.—JOINING WEAVERS

# WEAVING BEGUN

# CHAPTER III

# WEAVING BEGUN

---

## MODEL 1.—FIG. 4

### MAT WITH OPEN BORDER

MATERIAL

> 6 spokes No. 4 reed, 19 inches.
> 1 spoke No. 4 reed, 10 inches.
> 2 weavers No. 2 reed.
> 1 strand raffia.

Make an incision in the center of each of 4 spokes as illustrated in Fig. 1. Through these 4 spokes insert the other group of 4 spokes and the short spoke as in Fig. 1. You are now ready for the first step. Place a wet strand of raffia back of the 4 horizontal spokes; pass it over the group of 4 vertical spokes, back of the 5 horizontal spokes, over the lower 4 vertical spokes and back of the first group of horizontal spokes. Separate the groups of fours into groups of twos by bringing the raffia over 2 spokes, under 2 spokes, treating the short spoke as a separate group. Fig. 2. When two rows have been finished, the third and last step is made by weaving the raffia under 1 spoke and over the next,

37

thus separating each spoke. Fig. 3. After the
spokes are well separated, take a piece of No. 2
reed, place it back of a spoke and begin weaving
over 1 spoke, and back of the next one, until thirty-
two rows of weaving are completed. This will
make the mat about 5¾ inches in diameter. You
are now ready for the border.

OPEN BORDER NO. 1

Allow about 6½ inches for this border. This
border is made by placing each spoke back of the
next spoke to the right, and pushing it down by
the side of this spoke through the weaving.

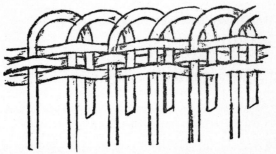

DIAGRAM NO. 14.—OPEN BORDER NO. 1

OPEN BORDER NO. 2

Open border No. 2 is made by bringing one spoke
back of the next two spokes to the right and push-

ing it well down through the weaving, by the side of the spoke.

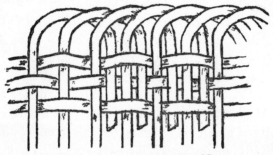

DIAGRAM NO. 15.—OPEN BORDER NO. 2

## MODEL 2.—FIG. 5

### MAT WITH CLOSED BORDER

MATERIAL

    8 spokes No. 4 reed, 19 inches.

    1 spoke No. 4 reed, 10 inches.

    1 ring No. oo reed.

    2 rings No. 2 blue reed.

    4 rings No. 2 natural reed.

After the spokes are arranged for weaving, take a short strand of oo reed, fasten and separate the spokes. Weave 1¾ inches with oo reed, then with No. 2 natural reed, weave six rows. Follow this with six rows of blue, then change to natural, and weave eleven rows natural, then with the blue reed, weave nine rows, change to natural, and finish the weaving with six rows of natural color reed.   Complete the mat with the following closed border:

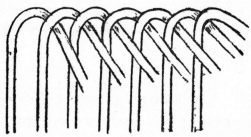

DIAGRAM No. 16.—CLOSED BORDER No. 1 (PART 1)

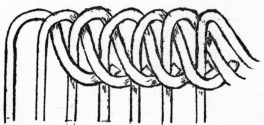

DIAGRAM No. 17.—CLOSED BORDER No. 1 (PART 2)

## CLOSED BORDER No. 1

Weaving to the right, carry one spoke back of the next spoke and out to the front; proceed in this way until every spoke is placed in this position.

The last spoke is pushed back and under the first
one. For the second row of this border, place the
first spoke, which had been brought back of the
second, in front of the third spoke and back of the
fourth spoke. Continue in this manner until the
row is finished. Be careful to draw all the spokes
tight, leaving just space enough for the preceding
spoke to pass through.

## MODEL 3.—FIG. 6

### BASKET FOR MOTHER'S BUTTONS

MATERIAL

    8 spokes No. 4 reed, 16 inches.
    1 spoke No. 4 reed, 9 inches.
    2 rings tan reed.
    2 rings natural color reed.
    1 strand of raffia.

The bottom of this basket is begun just like the
mat. After the spokes are separated with the
raffia, begin the weaving, and weave until a base
three inches is woven, then weave two rows with a
weaver of the tan reed. This completes the bottom of the basket. Wet the spokes well and with a
plier press them hard and turn them up. With the
same weaver continue the weaving until seven rows

have been woven up the side.   During the weaving hold the spokes firmly and straight.   Change the weave now to the natural color and work twelve rows, then with another ring of tan reed complete the weaving of the basket with nine rows.   Finish the basket with Open Border No. 2.

Bands of tan, combined with the natural color and woven over brown spokes, make a very pretty effect.

## MODEL 4.—FIG. 7

### BASKET FOR PENCILS

The second basket for the beginner is the pencil basket, much like the first, with sides higher and with a closed border.   This basket is woven all in the nautral color and then painted in gold.

MATERIAL

      6 spokes No. 4 reed, 15 inches.
      1 spoke No. 4 reed, 8 inches.
      4 No. 2 weavers.
      1 strand of raffia.

In a similar manner, as illustrated in Fig. 4, make a base 2¾ inches.   Turn the sides up sharply and weave 3½ inches.   Complete with Closed Border No. 1.

Fig. 5

Fig. 4

## MODEL 5.—FIG. 8

### BASKET FOR SPOOLS

This basket is woven in the natural color and afterwards dipped in brown dye. It makes a useful holder for spools.

MATERIAL

    8 spokes No. 3 reed, 14 inches.
    1 spoke No. 3 reed, 8 inches.
    Weavers No. 1 and No. 2 Reed.

With No. 1 reed, weave a base four inches. Press the spokes with the plier until soft. Turn them sharply upward and hold them straight. With No. 2 reed weave the sides $1\frac{3}{4}$ inches. With the spokes well soaked, press and hold them in towards the center of the basket. Continue the weaving, drawing the weaver tightly, until five rows are woven. Complete basket with the following border:

CLOSED BORDER NO. 2

For the first row of this border, place each spoke back of the next one, weaving to the right, and bring it out to the front. For the second row, each weaver is brought in front of the next 2 spokes and back of the next spoke or—numbering the spokes

1, 2, 3, 4, 5:—No. 1 spoke is brought back of No. 2 spoke, in front of the third and fourth spokes, and back of the fifth spoke, where it rests. Continue in this manner until all the spokes are woven in position. This border makes a decidedly pretty effect.

DIAGRAM No. 18.—CLOSED BORDER No. 2

## MODEL 6.—FIG. 9

### TOOTH-BRUSH HOLDER

This little curved basket is woven with brown reed over natural color spokes. The border is of the natural color reed being a continuation of the spokes.

MATERIAL

    8 spokes No. 3 reed, 15 inches.
    1 spoke No. 3 reed, 8 inches.
    Several rings No. 2 brown reed.
    1 strand brown raffia.

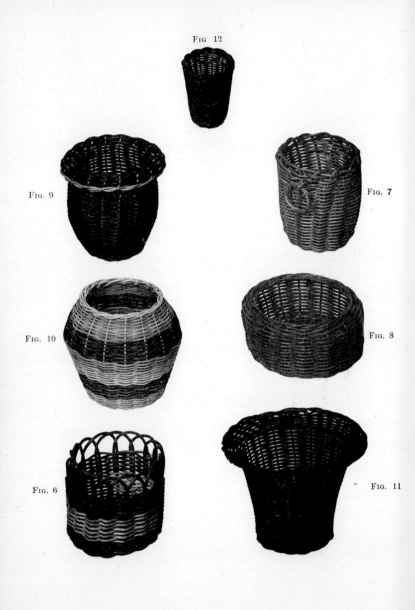

Fig 12

Fig. 9

Fig. 7

Fig. 10

Fig. 8

Fig. 6

Fig. 11

Weave the center of this basket with brown raffia to carry out the same effect as the brown reed.

Weave 1¼ inches with raffia. With a No. 2 brown weaver continue the weaving until a base 2½ inches is woven. After the sides are turned up, continue weaving up the sides, drawing the spokes gradually outward toward the weaver, until the basket measures 2½ inches high. Continue the weaving, drawing the weaver tightly and pressing the spokes in toward the center, until 1¾ inches more are woven. The basket should now have a slightly rounded effect. The diameter of basket should now be about three inches. The basket is curved outward in the following manner. Work the spokes outward and press them down toward the side of basket; hold firmly and continue the weaving in an easy manner. When nine rows of weaving are finished, complete the basket with Closed Border No. 1.

## MODEL 7.—FIG. 10

### BARREL SHAPED FANCY BASKET

This basket is woven over green spokes, with green bands about an inch from the top and bottom of basket. Green rings may be made for handle.

MATERIAL

    8 spokes No. 4 green reed, 20 inches.
    1 spoke No. 4 green reed, 11 inches.
    Weavers No. 2 natural.
    Weavers No. 2 green.
    1 strand green raffia.

Weave a center, and separate the spokes with green raffia. With No. 2 natural reed weave a base 3½ inches. Turn the sides up and drawing them outward weave ten rows. Change the reed to No. 2 green and holding the spokes in the same manner, weave a band of green ⅞ inch wide, then a band of the natural color 1½ inches wide.

Change the reed now to green. Hold the spokes well in toward the center and draw the weaver tightly. Work a band of green one inch and finish the weaving with one inch of natural reed. Complete the basket with the following closed border:

## CLOSED BORDER No. 3

As in the Closed Border No. 1 and No. 2, run each spoke back of the next spoke on the right and out to the front. The second row is woven by placing each spoke in front of the next three spokes to the right and back of the sixth. Weave each spoke in this way until the row is completed.

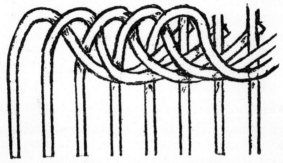

DIAGRAM NO. 19.—CLOSED BORDER NO. 3

## MODEL 8.—FIG. 11

### NO. 1 JARDINIERE

This flower pot covering basket is made of the natural reed. It may either be dipped in any shade of dye or stained. The one illustrated was dipped in dye when completed.

MATERIAL

    8 spokes No. 4 reed, 18 inches.
    1 spoke No. 4 reed, 10 inches.
    Weavers No. 2 reed.

Weave a bottom 4¼ inches. The sides are made by holding the spokes outward until 4½ inches are woven. This makes the diameter of the basket 4¾ inches. To obtain the outward slanting effect point the spokes straight out towards the weaver, and, after weaving four rows turn and hold the spokes slantingly upward. Finish this weave with six more rows. Complete the basket with the Closed Border No. 2.

## MODEL 9.—FIG. 12

### MATCH TRAY

This little basket may either be used for holding matches or tooth picks. It is woven in No. 2 natural reed over a small drinking glass, with No. oo as weaver. When finished, stain in old rose "Easy Dye" diluting the dye to get the tint desired.

MATERIAL

> 5 spokes No. 2 reed, 10½ inches.
> 1 spoke No. 2 reed, 6 inches.
> 2 Weavers No. oo reed.
> Handle—2 strands No. oo reed, 24 inches.

Weave a base 1⅛ inches with No. oo reed. Turn sharply upward and continue weaving until fifty-one rows of single weaving are woven. Be careful to keep the spokes straight and to weave closely. Complete the tray with Closed Border No. 1.

Make the ring handles one inch in diameter and attach to the basket under the border.

# SEPARATE BOTTOM BASKETS

## CHAPTER IV

## SEPARATE BOTTOM BASKETS

Separate bottom basket : the bottom of the basket is made separate from the sides, the latter being made by inserting spokes between the weaving, after the bottom is finished, and attaching them with an upsetting of three, four, or five rod coils. A bottom with an even number of spokes is woven with two weavers in pairing, or with three in triple twist.

### MODEL 10.—FIG. 13

#### DESK UTILITY BASKET

MATERIAL

    8 spokes No. 4 reed, 5 inches.
    31 spokes No. 2 reed, 10 inches.
    Weavers No. 2 Natural and No. 2 Green.

Make a bottom five inches. For the sides insert the thirty-one spokes in the bottom, one inch from edge. Place each spoke by the side of a base spoke. Turn up sharply and with three green weavers, make two rows of triple twist in this manner.

Place each of the three weavers back of a consecutive spoke, and beginning with the first weaver to the left, place it in front of the next two spokes to the right, back of the next spoke and then out to the front. Treat the other two weavers the same way, bringing each weaver in front of two spokes, back of one and out to the front. Continue this until two rows are woven.

With No. 2 natural reed weave 2½ inches, holding the spokes so as to get a very slight outward effect, then with thirteen rows of weaving, draw the spokes inward to obtain the rounded effect. Finish the weaving with two rows of triple twist in green, and complete the basket with the following border: First row, each spoke is placed back of the next spoke to the right and out; second row, each spoke is placed in front of three spokes to the right and in back of the next spoke, where it rests.

## MODEL 11.—FIG. 14

### COVERING FOR SMALL FLOWER POT

MATERIAL

       8 spokes No. 4 reed, 5 inches.
       34 spokes No. 2 reed, 18 inches.
       No. 2 natural reed used as weavers.
       No. 3 natural reed used in triple twist.

Over the 8 spoke center weave a base in pairing, 4½ inches in diameter. Separate 34 spokes in groups of twos, and considering each group of spokes as one spoke, insert them in base. One spoke in base will have a group placed each side of it, making 17 spokes. Attach the sides to base with an upset of two rows of rope twist. Work eighteen rows in double weave. The spokes are now flared slightly outward and five more rows complete the weaving.

The basket is finished off with No. 2 Closed Border. Continue the use of the two spokes as one throughout the border.

## MODEL 12.—FIG. 15

### STRIPED SEWING BASKET

The following three baskets are given to show how colored reed may be introduced and the effective result.

MATERIAL

> 10 spokes No. 4 brown reed, 5½ inches.
> 21 spokes No. 4 natural reed, 15 inches.
> Weavers No. 2 natural reed.
> Weavers No. 2 brown reed.
> Weavers No. 4 brown reed.
> Handle—2 pieces No. 5 brown reed, 8 inches.

Over a 10 spoke center, weave in pairing, six rows in natural color, change to brown and white, and weave four rows in pairing, change the weave to natural and complete the bottom which should be five inches in diameter. After inserting spokes for the sides, weave an upset in two rows of wale weave. Place a natural color weaver back of one spoke and weave one row around, stopping at the spoke where the weaving was begun; back of the spoke, to the right of the one, where the first weaver was placed, insert the brown weaver and weave around until the first weaver is reached. Continue this weave, first the natural then the brown, holding the spokes all the time slightly up and outward. Do this until thirty-eight rows of weaving are finished, nineteen of each color, alternating white and brown stripes. Finish the basket with two rows of triple twist and the following border. First row, each spoke is brought back of the one to the right and out, second row each spoke is brought in front of next three to the right and in back of the fourth spoke.

HANDLE

Place one end of an 8 inch spoke well down by the side of one of the spokes in the basket.

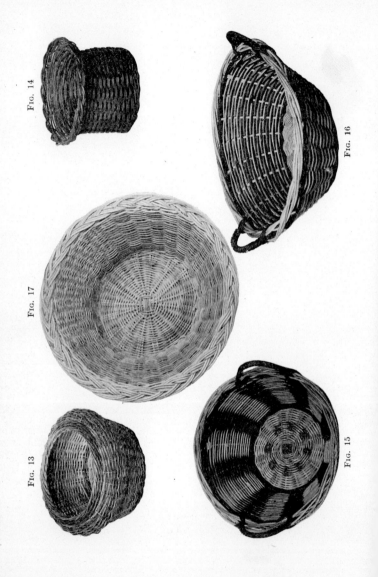

FIG. 14

FIG. 16

FIG. 17

FIG. 13

FIG. 15

Place the other end down the basket leaving about a three inch space between the ends. To the left of the handle place a brown weaver by the side of the inserted end of handle, bring it up over the handle on the outside, and weave three twists around the handle about an inch apart; bring the weaver over the handle to the inside of basket, down under the triple and out to the front. Follow the twist around the handle with the weaver until the handle is completely covered. End the weaver by bringing it up from the inside of the basket between the handle and down through the border and triple twist where it is lost amid the weaving.

## MODEL 13.—FIG. 16

### SEWING BASKET IN DOUBLE WEAVING

MATERIAL

10 spokes No. 4 natural reed, 5½ inches.
21 spokes No. 4 natural reed, 18 inches.
Weavers No. 2 natural reed.
Weavers No. 2 brown reed.
Weavers No. 4 brown reed.
Handle—2 pieces No. 5 brown reed, 8 inches.
3 weavers No. 2 brown reed.

Make a five inch base. Fasten the sides with an upset of two rows brown triple. The sides of this basket are woven in double weaving, one weaver of brown, the other of natural color. Eighteen rows of slewing with two rows of brown triple finish the weaving of the basket. Hold the spoke slightly out and up while weaving. Complete the basket with border described in preceding sewing basket. Handle is made as in preceding basket.

## MODEL 14.—FIG. 17
### SEWING BASKET IN CHECK EFFECT

MATERIAL

> 8 spokes No. 4 reed, 7 inches.
> 32 spokes No. 4 reed, 17 inches.
> Weavers No. 4 natural reed.
> Weavers No. 2 natural reed.
> Weavers No. 2 blue reed.

Make a base 6½ inches. Insert the spokes for sides and weave two rows of triple twist in No. 4 natural reed. The sides of this basket are woven in blue and white in the checker design, in the following way:

With No. 2 light blue reed, weave one row, stopping at the spoke to the left of where the weaver was inserted; back of this spoke, insert a natural color weaver and weave one row around meeting the first weaver. Continue the weaving now with the blue weaver, work in this way, first with blue reed, then with natural color, until eight rows are woven—you now have a striped effect of four rows in blue and four in white. In order to get the checker effect, the weave must now change. Bring each weaver back of two spokes at the end of the eighth row of weaving. If the weaving is correct the ninth row of weaving, which is in blue, will be woven under and over the same spokes as the eighth row, which is white. The ninth row is the beginning of the new group of weaving. Continue this weaving until you make five or six checks. The weaving should now be four rows of blue, four of white, four blue, four white, four blue, which gives a prominence to the blue, and makes a decidedly artistic piece of work.

During the weaving the spokes should be held in an outward direction. Follow this with two rows of triple twist and border described as follows:

*Commercial braid border*

### PLAITED BORDER

This border is especially appropriate for large baskets and trays. Allow thirteen inches for this border, spokes ¾ inch apart.

Insert 4 spokes which should be one inch longer than the spokes of the basket. Place each spoke by the side of each of 4 border spokes. This makes four groups of 2 spokes each. Number these groups 1, 2, 3, 4. Bend down towards the outside of basket No. 1, 2, 3 groups. Take No. 1 group pass it over Nos. 2 and 3 groups, in front of No. 4 group, and back of the next spoke which is No. 5 spoke. Bend down No. 4 group towards the outside of basket. Place No. 2 group over No. 3 and 4 groups, and back of No. 6 spoke. Bring No. 1 group, which is back of No. 5 spoke, to the outside of basket, by crossing it over No. 2 group between No. 5 and No. 6 spokes. Now bend down No. 5 spoke by the side of this group. Pass No. 3 group over the two groups on the outside of basket, and up between the two upright spokes. No. 2 group is brought to the outside of basket by crossing it over No. 3 group between No. 6 and No. 7 spokes. Bend down No. 6 spoke by the side of this group. No. 4 group is woven in same manner as No. 2 and 3. After the fourth group is woven, you should have one group of 2 spokes on the inside of basket and three groups of 3 spokes each on the outside of basket. Continue the border by weaving two of each group of 3 spokes, lying on outside of basket, over the next two groups on the outside of basket, in front of the first upright spoke, and back of the second where it rests until next group is woven.   The first inside group now is drawn to the outside of the basket by crossing it over this group between the two upright spokes.   The first upright spokes are always bent down to the outside of basket by the side of this group.   When all the groups are woven in this manner, there should be 1 spoke from each group facing the outside of basket, and four groups of 2 spokes each on the inside of basket where the border is completed.   Cut all the spokes closely.

The first three groups of spokes at the beginning of the border should not be drawn tight, enough space should be left to allow the last three groups of the border to pass through them easily.   The remainder of border should be woven tightly and close to the basket.

## MODEL 15.—FIG. 18

### GREEN AND WHITE BASKET

This little basket is a very convenient receptacle for holding loose threads or scraps while sewing.

MATERIAL

       8 spokes No. 4 natural reed, 5½ inches.
       31 spokes No. 2 natural reed, 10 inches.
       Weavers No. 3 green reed.
       Weavers No. 2 green reed.
       Weavers No. 2 natural reed.

Through an 8 spoke base, five inches wide, insert the 31 spokes. Weave two rows green triple, follow this in double weave using green and natural reed. Weave seven rows. Change to single weaving, using two weavers, and weave fourteen rows in the striped effect showing green and white stripe. Complete the weaving with two rows green in triple effect and the following border:

### Reversed Rope Border

Each spoke of the first row is brought back of the next spoke to the right and out. In the second row each spoke is brought back of the next spoke and out, showing a rope effect with spokes on outside.

## MODEL 16.—FIG. 19

### FANCY SEWING BASKET, NO. 1

The basket is woven, over a 16 spoke center, entirely of No. 2 reed. The spokes and triple twist are of brown reed while the remainder of the basket is woven in the natural color.

### Material

> 16 spokes No. 2 brown reed, 26 inches.
> Weavers No. 2 brown reed.
> Weavers No. 2 natural reed.

Fig. 20

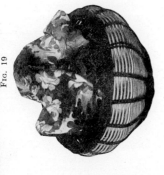

Fig. 19

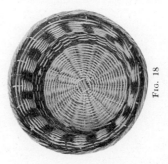

Fig. 18

Over the 16 spokes weave a base in pairing four inches in diameter. In the first three rows, consider each group of fours as one spoke, then separate the group of fours into groups of twos with seven rows of pairing. Consider each group of 2 spokes as 1 spoke throughout the base. The base should now be four inches in diameter. Turn the spokes with an upset of three rows of triple twist No. 2 brown reed.

Holding the spokes slightly up and outward, weave the basket two inches high. Now drawing the weaver tightly and pushing spokes inward toward center of basket weave twelve rows of single weaving. Finish with three rows of triple twist No. 2 brown reed. When this is completed take each spoke, and bring it out back of the next spoke to the right and down through the three rows of triple twist. Holding the spoke firmly, pass it through the three rows of triple twist at the base of the basket. Continue this with each group of spokes, which will show the striped effect on outside of basket. When all the spokes have been pulled through the triple twist at bottom of base, turn the basket upside down, and if the open border at the top of the basket is even, you are ready to complete the border at base of the basket. This border serves as a little stand for the basket.

## BORDER

Weaving to the right, each spoke is woven in front of the next spoke and back of the second spoke to the right where the end is cut off.

# HANDLES AND LIDS

# CHAPTER V

# HANDLES AND LIDS

## MODEL 17.—FIG. 21

### SMALL CARRYING BASKET IN STRIPED EFFECT

This little basket, in the striped design of blue and white with blue handle, was made by a little 10-year-old boy of the defective delinquent class.

MATERIAL

      6 spokes No. 4 natural reed, 20 inches.
      1 spoke No. 4 natural reed, 11 inches.
      Weavers No. 2 blue reed.
      Weavers No. 2 natural reed.
      Handle—1 spoke No. 4 natural reed, 20 inches.

Weave a base, with the striped design carried out, 2¾ inches. Two weavers are necessary to get this effect—one blue, the other of natural color. Weave these two colors in pairing. With the spokes slightly flared outward, weave the sides, in the striped effect, 3½ inches. With two weavers of blue and one of natural, weave two rows of "Wale." Finish with Open Border No. 2.

HANDLE

Insert one end of the 20 inch spoke of No. 4 reed down through the weaving, to the right of one of the spokes of the basket.   Insert the other end on the opposite side of basket in the same way.   Place the end of a blue weaver down, through the weaving, by the side of inserted spoke, twist it over the handle, then under, then over, next under, over, until the end of the handle is reached, thus making nine twists around the handle.   The last twist is passed back of the handle, over the triple twist to the inside of the basket, then it is brought to the outside of basket under the triple twist.   Following the twists around the handle, the weaver is twirled in this way until the handle is completely covered by the blue weaver.   Four rows of this weaving around the basket will cover the entire handle.   To fasten the end of the weaver, carry it back of the spoke, between the woven handle, and down through the triple twist, where it is made secure and then cut off.

## MODEL 18.—FIG. 22

### LITTLE MARKETING BASKET IN GREEN

This may be used in gathering eggs from the chicken yard or in doing little marketing.   It is all

woven in natural color reed and after the basket is
completed is dyed.

MATERIAL

> 10 spokes No. 4 reed, 23 inches.
> 1 spoke No. 4 reed, 12 inches.
> Weavers No. 4 natural reed.
> Weavers No. 2 natural reed.
> Handle—1 spoke No. 5 reed, 26 inches.

Over 10½ spokes weave a base five inches in
diameter. Turn up with three rows of No. 4 reed
in triple twist. In single weaving, work the sides
five inches high giving a slightly rounded effect and
widening toward the top. Finish with three rows
of triple and the following border.

Numbering the spokes 1, 2, 3, 4, 5, 6, 7, take No.
1 spoke back of No. 2, in front of No. 3, back of No.
4, in front of No. 5, back of No. 6 where it rests;
then No. 2 spoke follows in the same way, back of
No. 3, in front of No. 4, back of No. 5, in front of
No. 6, back of No. 7, where it rests. Each spoke
is woven in the same manner until all spokes have
disappeared amid the weaving.

## HANDLE

To make the handle firm and strong, insert the
ends four and a half inches through the weaving

of the basket. The handle is entirely covered with
No. 2 reed as described in preceding basket.

## MODEL 19.—FIG. 23

### LUNCH BASKET WITH LID

MATERIAL

    10 spokes No. 4 reed, 4 inches.
    19 spokes No. 4 reed, 13 inches.
    Handle—1 strand No. 5 reed, 20 inches.
    Lid—8 spokes No. 4 reed, 18 inches.
    Weavers No. 4 reed.
    Weavers No. 2 reed.

Weave a base four inches. Work the sides four
inches high. Both the top and bottom of the sides
are woven with two rows No. 4, triple twist. Finish
with the following border. Number the spokes 1,
2, 3, 4, 5, 6, 7, 8. Turn down the first four toward
the outside of the basket. Place No. 1 spoke back
of No. 2, No. 2 spoke back of No. 3, No. 3 spoke
back of No. 4, No. 4 spoke back of No. 5; now
bring No. 1 spoke over No. 2 and No. 3 spokes,
in front of No. 5 spoke, over No. 4 spoke, back of
No. 6 spoke. Carry No. 5 spoke back of No. 6
spoke and place it by the side of No. 1 spoke. In
like manner, run No. 2 spoke over No. 3 and No. 4
spokes, in front of No. 6 spoke, over No. 5 spoke

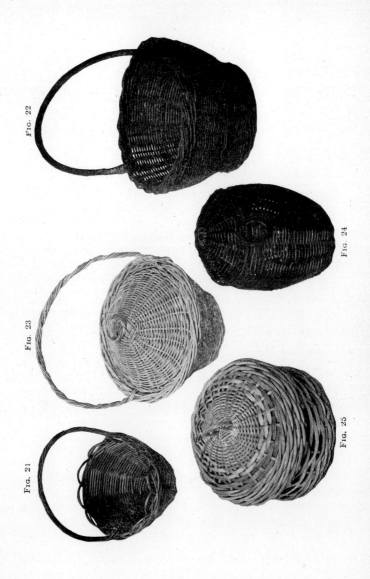

FIG. 22

FIG. 24

FIG. 23

FIG. 21

FIG. 25

and back of No. 7 spoke. Place No. 6 spoke back of No. 7 spoke and bring it out to the front by the side of No. 2 spoke. Continue in this manner until all the spokes are woven in the proper position. Be careful to make the border uniform throughout. The diameter of the top of basket should now measure 6¾ inches.

DIAGRAM NO. 20.—HEAVY BORDER

The handle is not completely covered, like the preceding basket, but a small part of the foundation is shown between the twists.

The lid is made similar to that in the preceding lesson except on a larger scale. It should fit closely within the basket. The base when finished should measure 6¾ inches. It is finished off with a Rope Twist Border. The handle of the lid is a twisted ring made as described in the preceding chapter.

## MODEL 20.—FIG. 24

### OVAL BASKET WITH LID

MATERIAL

    6 spokes No. 3 reed, 21 inches.
    1 spoke No. 3 reed, 11 inches.
    Weavers No. 2 reed.
    Lid—6 spokes No. 3 reed, 12 inches.
    1 spoke No. 3 reed, 7 inches.
    Weavers No. 2 reed.

On a three inch base, weave a slightly rounded basket five inches high. Finish with Closed Border No. 2.

In making a lid for a basket the first thing to be decided on is its shape; if the basket is barrel shaped, the lid to harmonize should have the curved effect. The lid of this basket is rounded to correspond with the basket.

LID

Weave a good center, over the 6½ spokes, with either raffia or No. 00 reed. After ¾ inch is woven, begin with fine No. 2 reed, and weave two rows, drawing the spokes in with the weaver. After two rows are woven, hold the spokes slightly outward and weave fourteen rows. Complete the basket with the following border which is suitable for lids of baskets:

## Rope Twist Border

Each spoke is passed in front of the next spoke to the right and brought inside the lid. For the second row, each spoke is passed to the outside of the lid over the next spoke to the right, and to the inside of the lid where it is cut off carefully.

The ring handle is made in the following way:

With a strand of No. 2 reed, 17 inches long, make a ring about one inch; then weaving alternately with one end and then the other, pass the ends in and out around the ring—two rows complete the ring. When the ring is finished you should have ends about 3½ inches long. These ends are fastened above two rows of the weaving in the lid, thus securing the ring to the lid.

After the lid is placed in proper position on the basket, it is fastened by holding the ring down by side of the basket and placing the center of a strand of No. 2 reed back of a spoke in the basket. Draw both ends out, and in the form of a cross, pass them over the lower part of ring, draw them under the weaving to the inside of the basket where they are woven in and out to make them secure.

The rings for the front of basket and lid are made in a similar way, the ends being woven in and out amid the weaving of the basket and lid. One ring should be smaller than the other to keep the larger ring from slipping out.

## MODEL 21.—FIG. 25

### CANDY BASKET

MATERIAL

    10 spokes No. 5 reed, 6 inches.
    20 spokes No. 5 reed, 8 inches.
    Lid—10 spokes No. 5 reed, 15 inches.
    1 spoke No. 5 reed, 8 inches.
    Weavers Nos. 00, 2, 5 round reed.
    Weavers No. 5 oval reed.

Weave a 6 inch base. Turn the sides with three rows of No. 5, triple twist. With oval reed No. 5, weave 7 rows in the two and one weave, change to No. 5 reed and finish with three rows triple. While weaving, the spokes should be slightly drawn in. The following border is used: first row each spoke is run back of one spoke and out to the front; second row, each spoke is passed in front of the next two spokes and in back of the third where it is cut off. Diameter of top of base should be almost five and a half inches.

FIG. 26

LID

The center of lid corresponding to center in the base of the basket is woven and separated with No. ∞ reed. Weave twelve rows of No. 2 reed next. Then with oval reed No. 5, weave in single weaving, five rows. Hold the spokes, to get a slightly rounded effect. Turn down the spokes with four rows of triple twist. Finish the basket with the Rope Twist Border, described under Model 20. The diameter of the lid should be a little over 6 inches. It should fit the basket so as to slide off and on easily. The ring handle in the center completes the lid.

## MODEL 22.—FIG. 26

### FANCY SEWING BASKET WITH LID

MATERIAL

    10 spokes No. 4 reed, 5½ inches.
    21 spokes No. 4 reed, 16 inches.
    Lid—16 spokes No. 4 reed, 18 inches.
    1 spoke No. 4 reed, 7 inches.
    Weavers No. 2 reed and No. 4 reed.
    Handle—1 spoke No. 2 reed, 21 inches.

Over the 10 spokes, weave a base 5½ inches. Insert the 21 spokes and turn them up with two rows of triple twist. Hold the spokes slantingly outward and weave the sides 4¾ inches high. Finish with three rows triple twist and the following border:

## BORDER

Numbering the spokes 1 to 7 and weaving to the right, place No. 1 spoke back of No. 2, No. 2 spoke back of No. 3, No. 3 spoke back of No. 4, No. 4 spoke back of No. 5. Now take No. 1 spoke, place it in front of Nos. 3 and 4 spokes and back of No. 5. Place No. 2 spoke in front of Nos. 4 and 5 spokes and back of No. 6 spoke. No. 3 spoke is passed in front of Nos. 5 and 6 spokes and back of No. 7. Continue this weaving until border is finished.

## LID

Arrange the 16 spokes as described in Chapter II.

Weave three rows in pairing, and separate the spokes into groups of twos. Hold the spokes slightly curved and weave twelve rows in pairing. Insert the one seven inch spoke and weave one row triple twist. Now hold the spokes almost straight and continue weaving until a diameter of 9¼ inches is obtained. Complete the lid with a rope border.

Attach a ring handle to the lid as shown in the model.

# HANGING BASKETS

## CHAPTER VI
## HANGING BASKETS

If it is possible to add more beauty to nature in the arranging of flowers and vines, etc., the use of the various and wonderfully attractive hanging baskets that can easily be made will afford the opportunity. The harmonious selection of flowers to combine harmoniously with the color of the basket is open to the artist and craftsman. The opportunity is wide for originality in the making of these baskets. The basket maker finds himself flooded with so many ideas that it is impossible to put them in book form. The following are a few suggestions.

### MODEL 23.—FIG. 27
### SMALL GREEN HANGING BASKET

MATERIAL

    8½ spokes No. 4 reed, 27 inches.
    Handle—1 spoke No. 5 reed, 27 inches.
    Weavers No. 2 reed.

Weave a four inch base. Turn up with three rows 3 coil weave. Holding the sides slightly outward weave twenty-six rows, then holding the spokes slightly inward and drawing the weaver tight, work twenty-six rows. Complete the basket with three rows of triple twist and the following border: First row, each spoke passes back of one spoke and out to the front; second row, each spoke is brought in front of two spokes and in back of the next spoke.

HANDLE

Place an end of the No. 5-27 inch spoke through the triple twist at bottom of basket, bring it up through the triple twist at top of basket; do the same on the opposite side of the basket. When the handle is thus arranged, with two rows of No. 2 reed make a twisted handle. Arrange the twists about an inch and a half apart.

Figs. 28 and 29 are small flower receptacles. They are both woven over No. 4 reed.

MODEL 24.—FIG. 30

NO. 2 BOWL SHAPED HANGING BASKET

This basket is worked with No. 2 reed as foundation and No. 1 reed as the weaver.

MATERIAL

8½ spokes No. 2 reed, 21 inches.
Handle—1 spoke No. 5 reed, 28 inches.
Weavers No. 2 reed.

This little basket has a three inch base.   Hold the spokes straight and weave the sides about one inch, single weaving.   Bend the spokes out and weave two inches.   Hold the spokes in toward the center of basket and draw the weaver tight; in this position weave two more inches.   Follow this with two rows of triple twist in No. 2 reed, and the border described under Model 20.

## HANDLE

Insert the ends of the handles two inches below the top of basket.   Bring them inside the basket back of eighteen rows of weaving, draw them to the outside of basket and down in front of sixteen rows of weaving.   Bring the ends through the weaving to the inside of basket.   Fasten the ends securely to the basket by weaving a strand of No. 2 reed in and out in the form of a cross.   With one ring of No. 1 reed, make a twisted handle, allowing two inch space between each twist; the second row of handle is made by making another twist around the handle, the twist being made in the middle of the intervening spaces, showing a separate woven twist all way around and having a spacing of one inch between each twist.

## MODEL 25.—FIG. 31

### NO. 3 HANGING BASKET

This basket is made large enough to allow a large glass to slip in and out easily.

MATERIAL

        10½ spokes No. 5 reed, 24 inches.
        Handle—1 piece No. 6 reed, 39 inches.
        Weavers No. 4 reed.
        Weavers No. 5 oval reed.
        Weavers No. oo reed.

A base 4½ inches is woven in the following manner: six rows of single weaving of No. oo reed separate the spokes. Follow this with five rows of triple twist in No. oo reed, four rows of single weaving in oval reed and one row No. 4 reed in triple twist. Turn the sides up with four more rows of triple twist. With oval reed, weave twelve rows of single weaving. Hold the spokes well in and draw the weaver tightly. The diameter of basket should now be 2¾ inches wide. Continue the weaving, drawing the spokes well out and holding the weaver loosely. The basket should have eighteen rows of oval weaving. Follow this with three rows of triple twist and the following border: first row, each spoke is passed back of one spoke and out; second

FIG. 30

FIG. 31

FIG. 28

FIG. 29

FIG. 27

row, each spoke is brought in front of three spokes and in back of the next one.

HANDLE

Insert the ends of handle through the four rows of triple twist at the base of basket. The ends must be inserted just opposite to each other. Place a strand of oval reed to the right of inserted handle and between the third and fourth rows of triple weave. Draw the weaver first over the handle, then under the handle. About two inches above where the handle is inserted, pass the weaver over the handle and carry it to inside of basket, under the border. Twist the weaver around the handle twenty-one times. Pass it down under the border to the outside of basket; three more twists complete one row of the handle.

Now run the weaver to inside of basket, between the third and fourth rows of triple twist, cross, and bring to outside of basket at the left of handle. The weave is continued around the handle, forming a cross at every twist in the handle.

6

## MODEL 26.—FIG. 32

### BASKET WITH BRAIDED HANDLE

**MATERIAL**

    8 spokes No. 4 reed, 5 inches.
    17 spokes No. 3 reed, 11 inches.
    Handle—3 pieces No. 4 reed, 40 inches.
    Weavers No. 4 reed.
    Weavers No. 2 reed.

Through a five-inch base, insert 17 spokes. Weave an upset of three rows of triple twist. To get the desired shape weave twenty-two rows, single weaving, holding the spokes inward. Now hold the spokes out and weave twenty-eight rows. With four weavers, placing each weaver back of a corresponding spoke, weave two rows; each weaver in turn is brought in front of three spokes and back of one. Finish with the following border:

First row, pass each spoke back of one spoke and out; second row, each spoke is carried in front of three spokes and in back of the next one.

For the handle, insert the three pieces No. 4 reed just above the triple twist at the base of basket. Make two twists and pass remainder of reed through the upper eight rows of weaving and lower two rows of triple weave. Braid the reed twenty-

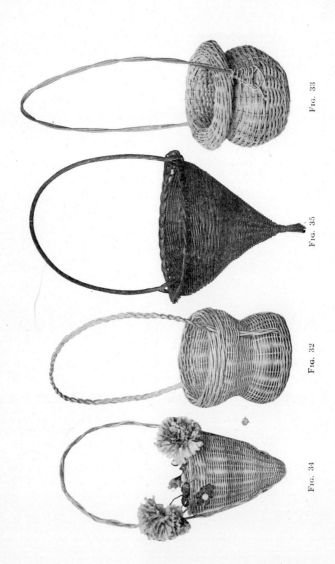

FIG. 33

FIG. 35

FIG. 32

FIG. 34

four inches. The ends are now inserted through the lower two rows of triple weaving and the upper eight rows of single weaving. With two more twists the ends are carried inside the basket just above the triple weave, and there made secure.

## MODEL 27.—FIG. 33

### BOWL SHAPED WITH FLARED TOP

MATERIAL

    10½ spokes No. 4 reed, 27 inches.
    Handle—2 pieces No. 5 reed, 35 inches.
    Weavers No. 2 reed.
    Weavers No. 4 reed.

The base of this basket is four inches. The sides are woven in double weaving, having a decided rounded effect. The flare at the top is made by bending the spokes down the outside of basket. An inch and a half of flare is woven. Complete with two rows of triple and the following border: Hold the basket upside down and weave to right, in front of one spoke and over two spokes. The sides of this basket are 2½ inches high.

About half way down the sides of the basket, insert the ends of the handle through four rows of weaving, the ends to be 1¾ inches apart. The ends are fastened securely by weaving in and out and across the spokes; the weaving is continued under and over the handle until the top of basket is reached; here the handle is made secure by carrying a weaver over the handle, and working it in and out through the weaving of the basket. Make twenty-eight inches of coil with the two spokes. Fasten the handle, in a similar manner, on the opposite side.

## MODEL 28.—FIG. 34

### FUNNEL SHAPED HANGING BASKET

MATERIAL

> 8½ spokes No. 2 reed, 31 inches.
> 1 piece No. 6 reed, 36 inches.
> Weavers No. oo reed.
> Weavers No. 2 reed.
> Weavers No. 4 reed.

After fastening the spokes with No. oo reed, weave five rows of single weaving. Change the weaver to No. 2 reed and work twenty-three rows in single weaving, holding the spokes in towards center. Continue the weaving until fifty-seven rows are woven. With No. 4 reed, make four rows triple twist and complete the basket with border described under Model 22.

When finished, the diameter at top of basket should measure 5½ inches.

HANDLE

Insert the ends of handle two inches from bottom. With No. ∞ reed fasten the ends to basket with the tie bow effect, then finish the handle in a twisted design.

FIG. 35

The funnel basket under Fig. 35 is dyed in dark green. It makes an attractive basket for cut flowers and vines. It is made of No. 4 and No. 2 reed. The handle from No. 5 reed.

# FLOWER RECEPTACLES

# CHAPTER VII

## FLOWER RECEPTACLES

### MODEL 29.—FIG. 36

#### VASE WITH HANDLES

**MATERIAL**

8 spokes No. 2 reed, 22 inches.
1 spoke No. 2 reed, 12 inches.
Handle—2 spokes No. 2 reed, 20 inches.
2 spokes No. 4 reed, 20 inches.
Weavers No. 2 reed.

This covering may be woven over a small vase or a pint jar.

Over the 8½ spokes weave a base 2¾ inches. Pinch the spokes sharply and turn up with three rows of triple twist in No. 2 reed. Weave around the jar in single weaving, until forty-four rows are completed. For the handle place the centers of one piece of No. 4 reed and one piece No. 2 reed between the 42nd and 43rd rows of weaving, twist the No. 4 reed around in a plain coil and carry the No. 2 reed around this coil. Do the same on the opposite side for the other handle. Form the oval handle, as seen in picture, and secure the four ends of each handle in place by fastening them to jar with a fine cord which may be pulled out later. Weave twenty-nine more rows in single weaving. Complete and fasten the handle with five rows triple twist. To prevent the handle from loosening or falling out, the triple twist should be woven over and under the ends of the handles. The following border completes the vase:

First row, each spoke is placed back of the spoke to the right and out.

Second row, each spoke is brought in front of the spoke to the right and in where it is cut off closely.

## MODEL 30.—FIG. 37

### NO. 2 GREEN JARDINIERE

MATERIAL

     8 spokes No. 4 reed, 5½ inches.
     34 spokes No. 2 reed, 17 inches.
     Weavers No. 4 reed.
     Weavers No. 2 reed.

Over an 8 spoke foundation, weave a base five inches. Insert the 34 spokes, considering two spokes as one, making 17 spokes. Turn up with three rows triple twist. In double weaving, work

FIG. 43

FIG. 36

FIG. 42

FIG. 36

FIG. 41

fifteen rows, holding the spokes outward toward the weaver. This will make the basket three inches high. Now holding the spokes well inward, weave fifteen rows in double weaving. The basket is now 5¼ inches high. Complete the sides of the basket with three rows triple twist. Finish with the following border:

First row, each spoke is brought back of next spoke and out.

Second row, each spoke is brought in front of next two spokes and in.

Third row, each spoke is brought over next spoke and in back of the next where it rests.

## MODEL 31.—FIG. 38

### NO. 3 JARDINIERE, IN OVAL REED

MATERIAL

  10 spokes No. 5 reed, 25 inches.
  Weavers No. oo reed.
  Weavers No. 1 reed.
  Weavers No. 5 reed.
  Weavers No. 5 oval reed.

After inserting 5 spokes through the other 5 spokes, fasten in cross form with No. oo reed. Weave seven rows with No. oo reed, separating the

spokes. With No. 1 reed, weave seven more rows.
Follow this with six rows of No. 5 split reed. Work
one coil of triple twist with No. 5 reed. This makes
a base six inches. Pinch the spokes sharply and
turn up with four rows of No. 5 triple. Hold the
spokes slantingly inward and weave seventeen rows
of No. 5 oval reed. The diameter should be 5½
inches. Bend the spokes outward in a curved
effect and weave four rows in No. 5 triple. Complete with the following border:

First row, each spoke is passed back of one spoke
and out. Second row, carry each spoke in front of
three spokes and in.


## MODEL 32.—FIG. 39

### JARDINIERE FOR RUBBER PLANT

MATERIAL

> 8 spokes No. 5 reed, 6 inches.
> 31 spokes No. 5 reed, 18 inches.
> Weavers No. 2 reed.
> Weavers No. 4 reed.

Weave a base 5½ inches. Insert spokes and
turn up with four rows of triple twist No. 4 reed.
Follow this with twelve rows of double weaving,
three rows of three-rod coil in No. 2 reed, ten rows

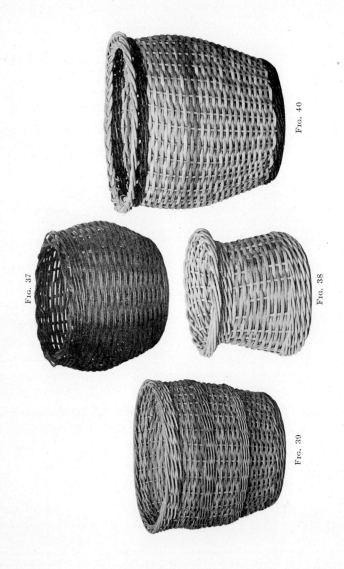

FIG. 40

FIG. 37

FIG. 38

FIG. 39

of double weaving, four rows of three-rod coil No. 2 reed, nine rows of double weaving and three rows of three-rod coil. Complete with border described under Model 22.

After the basket is finished, dye it a dark brown or green.

## MODEL 33.—FIG. 40
### OVAL REED JARDINIERE

MATERIAL

      8 spokes No. 5 reed, 8 inches
      31 spokes No. 5 reed, 25 inches.
      Weavers No. 4 brown reed.
      Weavers No. 5 oval reed.

Over an 8 spoke foundation, weave a base 7¾ inches. Insert 31 spokes and set up three rows of No. 4 brown reed in triple twist. The spokes are held slantingly outward until twenty-five rows of No. 5 oval or split reed are woven. Weave seventeen rows in No. 5 oval reed, holding the spokes curved in towards the center of basket. Complete the basket with three rows triple twist No. 4 brown reed, and the plaited border.

## MODEL 34.—FIG. 41

### FERN DISH

**MATERIAL**

    8 spokes No. 2 reed, 5½ inches.
    61 spokes No. 2 reed, 16 inches.
    Weavers No. 2 reed.

This fern dish basket is woven over a small white enamel dish:

Weave a base 5½ inches. Insert 2 spokes by the side of each base spoke. Consider each group of 2 spokes as 1 spoke. Turn up with two rows of triple twist. Place the dish in the basket and, while weaving around the dish, hold the spokes straight and draw the weaver tight. Weave twenty-nine rows. Curve the spokes over the dish and weave four more rows, single weaving, and two rows of triple twist in No. 2 reed.

Now bring each group of spokes back of the next two groups, out to the front, through the triple twist and down through the triple twist at the base of basket. When all the groups have been brought through the triple twist at the base, turn the basket upside down, and weave the following border for a stand for the dish:

Weaving to the right, each group is brought back

of the next two groups and out to the front; second row, each group is placed in front of the next spoke and in back of the next where it is clipped off.

## Fig. 42

This basket is woven in a similar manner to Fig. 41. The spokes are of No. 2 natural reed, while the weavers are No. 2 light brown reed. The border, the outside spokes and the stand are of natural reed. This combination makes a strikingly attractive basket.

## Fig. 43

This flower basket is dyed after it is made and then waxed. The shape may be molded to accommodate any purpose.

# OVAL BASKETS

# CHAPTER VIII
## OVAL BASKETS

### MODEL 35.—FIG. 44

#### NO. 1 OVAL BASKET WITH ROUND BASE

MATERIAL

> 8 spokes No. 5 reed, 5½ inches.
> 39 spokes No. 5 reed, 26 inches.
> Handle—2 spokes No. 5 reed, 35 inches.
> Weavers No. 2 reed.
> Weavers No. 5 reed.

Weave a base five inches. Insert the 39 spokes, pinch sharply and turn upward. Make secure with three rows No. 5 reed in triple twist. Weave an inch with No. 2 reed, holding all spokes straight. Now continue the weaving by holding the side spokes straight and the end spokes down and out towards the weaver. Continue the weaving in this manner until seventy rows of simple weaving, and three rows triple twist No. 5 reed, are made. Finish with the following border:

First row, each spoke is placed back of two spokes and out.

Second row, each spoke is placed in front of two spokes and in.

Handle

Insert the two pieces No. 5 reed and weave a twisted handle as shown in Fig. 44.

## MODEL 36.—FIG. 45

### NO. 2 OVAL BASKET (IN GREEN AND BROWN)

Material

    10 spokes No. 5 reed, 5½ inches.
    20 spokes No. 5 brown reed, 28 inches.
    19 spokes No. 5 brown reed, 15 inches.
    Handle—1 spoke No. 8 brown reed, 32 inches.
    Weavers No. 2 green reed.
    Weavers No. 4 brown reed.
    Weavers No. 2 brown reed.

Weave a five inch base. Insert the spokes, pinch, and turn sharply upward with three rows of brown No. 4 triple. In pairing, weave with No. 2 green reed, twenty-three rows. Insert 19 spokes and weave three rows triple No. 3 green. Follow this with forty-one rows green reed, in single weaving, and three rows No. 4 brown reed, in triple. Complete with the rope border.

The spokes should be held straight and firm until

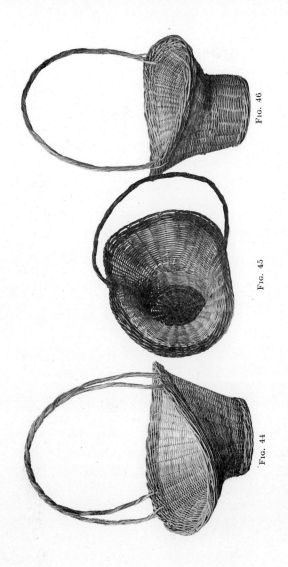

Fig. 46

Fig. 45

Fig. 44

three inches of weaving are finished; then the ends are spread out and bent down towards the base of basket until the rest of the weaving is completed, Fig. 45.

When completed the sides should measure seven inches.

HANDLE.

Push the ends of handle well down amid the weaving. Weave six rows of coil, with No. 2 brown reed, around the handle.

FIG. 46.

This basket is made from the natural reed. A rounded effect is woven for about three inches up the sides, the end spokes are then flared out. A single spoke of No. 6 reed is used for the handle.

## OVAL BASES
### MODEL 37.—FIG. 49
#### NO. 1 OVAL BASE

MATERIAL

>   3 spokes No. 4 reed, 7 inches.
>   5 spokes No. 4 reed, 5 inches.
>   Weavers No. 2 reed.

Split each of the five spokes in the center and pass the 3 spokes through them—Fig. 47.

The 5 spokes should be arranged in horizontal positions about ¾ inch apart, the end spokes about two inches from the end of the base spokes. Fig. 47. The base is woven in pairing. Place No. 1 weaver back of No. 1 spoke, No. 2 weaver back of No. 2 spoke. Fig. 48. Pass No. 1 weaver over No. 2 spoke, back of No. 3 spoke; No. 2 weaver crosses over No. 1 weaver to the front of base, which is the side facing the weaver, passes in front of No. 3 spoke and out back of No. 4. Fig. 48. No. 1 weaver crosses No. 4 spoke and out back of No. 5 spoke and so on around the base. The group of three base spokes are treated as one spoke until two rows have been woven. They are then separated and woven as single spokes. Fig. 49.

## MODEL 38.—FIG. 53

### NO. 2 OVAL BASE

MATERIAL

    3 spokes No. 4 reed, 8 inches.
    7 spokes No. 4 reed, 5 inches.
    Weavers No. 2 brown reed.
    Weavers No. 2 natural reed.

Arrange the seven spokes in a horizontal position on the three base spokes. The spokes arranged ½ inch apart. The end spokes double. Fig. 50.

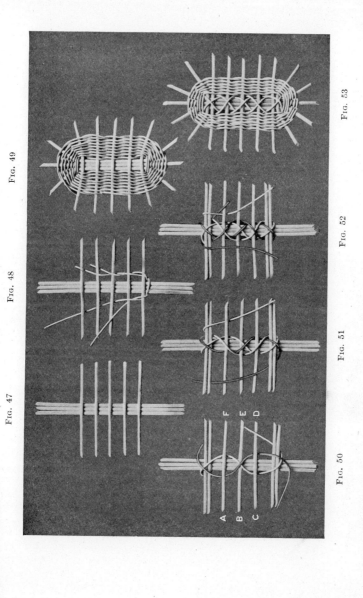

FIG. 49

FIG. 48

FIG. 47

FIG. 53

FIG. 52

FIG. 51

FIG. 50

Take the center of a single weaver, or using two strands of different colors, place it or them under the upper three base spokes and back of the upper end spokes. Take the left hand weaver, or the natural one, over the end spokes, down under F, up over B-E, under C and up over to the right where it crosses over the end spokes. Fig. 50.

Now take the brown weaver, which is back of the upper base spokes, bring it over the upper end spokes under A, over B-E, under D, over the lower end spokes. Fig. 50.

Return to weaver No. 1, cross it over C-D, under B, cross over A-F, and under the upper left end spokes. Fig. 51. Bring No. 2 or brown weaver, under the lower left end spokes, cross over C-D, under E, cross over A-F, under the upper end spokes over the upper three base spokes. Fig. 52. Finish your base in pairing, as shown in Fig. 53.

## MODEL 39.—FIG. 54

### CARD TRAY

This tray is made by combining blue and natural color reed.

MATERIAL

    3 spokes No. 4 reed, 7 inches.
    5 spokes No. 4 reed, 4 inches.
    32 spokes No. 4 reed, 14 inches.
    Weavers No. 2 blue reed.
    Weavers No. 2 natural reed.

Through the five spokes place the three 7-inch spokes. Arrange each of the five spokes ¾ inch apart. Fasten the spokes in place with two rows of pairing, combining the blue and natural reed. Separate the end spokes with eight rows of pairing, carrying the striped effect throughout. Insert 32 spokes No. 4 reed, placing a spoke by the side of each spoke in the base. Turn sharply upward and weave one row of triple twist in No. 4 reed. With blue and white weavers, weave nine rows in pairing, carrying the striped effect up the sides. Hold the spokes while weaving slightly outward. Finish with one row of triple twist and plaited border.

## MODEL 40.—FIG. 55

### OVAL BASE BASKET

MATERIAL

    4 spokes No. 5 reed, 7 inches.
    7 spokes No. 5 reed, 4 inches.
    29 spokes No. 4 reed, 16 inches.
    Handle—1 piece No. 5 reed, 20 inches.
    Weavers No. 2 natural reed.
    Weavers No. 4 brown reed.
    3 yards braided straw.

Slip the four spokes through the seven spokes. Arrange the seven spokes ½ inch apart.

Weave a base over this 7 inches long, 4 inches wide. Insert the twenty-nine spokes. Pinch and turn sharply upward. Set up two rows triple twist in No. 4 brown reed. Weave seven rows of braided straw and complete the sides with two rows of triple twist in No. 4 brown reed. The following border is used:

First row, each spoke is placed back of next spoke to right. Second row, each spoke is placed in front of next two spokes to right and in back of the next spoke. The ends of handle are inserted between the border, through the triple twist and down between the braiding. The handle is woven as described under Model 18.

## MODEL 41.—FIG. 56

### NO. 1 OVAL BASE FLOWER BASKET

MATERIAL

　　3 spokes No. 5 reed, 6½ inches.
　　7 spokes No. 5 reed, 4 inches.
　　27 spokes No. 4 reed, 14 inches.
　　27 spokes No. 4 reed, 20 inches.
　　4 spokes No. 4 reed, 12 inches.
　　Weavers No. 2 reed.
　　Weavers No. 4 reed.
　　Handle—3 spokes No. 6 reed, 33 inches.

In pairing, weave a base 6 inches long 3¾ inches wide. Insert the 27 20-inch spokes, and turn up with four rows of triple twist. While weaving the basket, hold the end spokes out toward the weaver, the side spokes straight.

Work the basket 3¾ inches in single weaving with No. 3 reed. Now insert the 27 14-inch spokes, placing a spoke by the side of each spoke in the basket. Weave five rows of 3-coil weave in No. 5 reed.

Place the four spokes for the border. Complete the basket with the plaited border.

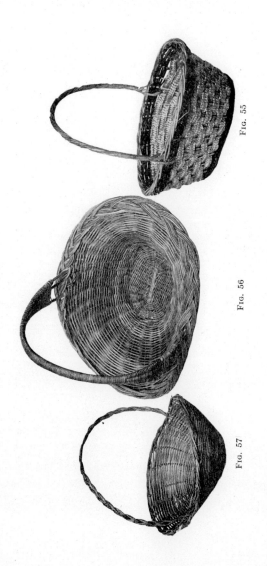

FIG. 55

FIG. 56

FIG. 57

## Handle

Place the ends of the handle through the border, down about 2½ or 3 inches in the weaving. Measure 7 inches, from the border of the basket, up the handle. Beginning here, with fine No. 1 reed, make a continuation coil around the handle of basket until it is 7 inches from the end of the handle on the opposite side. Now separate each piece of reed, and in simple weaving, weave the remainder of the handle over one spoke, under one, until it is 1½ inches from border of basket. Fasten the end of the weaver up between the weaving.

To make the handle secure, fasten, in double cross form, each end of the handle to the sides of basket.

## Fig. 57

This little basket is useful when gathering flowers. It is made entirely of No. 2 reed, and is finished with a braided handle.

# TRAYS

# CHAPTER IX

## TRAYS

### MODEL 42.—FIG. 58

#### PIN TRAY

MATERIAL

16 spokes No. 2 reed, 15 inches.
Weavers No. 2 reed.

Over the 16 spoke foundation weave four rows in pairing. Separate the groups of fours into groups of twos and weave six rows in pairing. The base should measure four inches. Turn the spokes sharply upward. Consider throughout the weaving each group of twos as one spoke.

Weave two rows No. 2 reed in three rod coil. Hold the spokes to secure a slight outward slant and weave seven rows in pairing. Finish the tray with following border:

First row, each spoke is passed back of next spoke and out.

Second row, each spoke is passed in front of next spoke and in.

## MODEL 43.—FIG. 59

### CANDY TRAY NO. 1

**MATERIAL**

> 16 spokes No. 2 reed, 24 inches.
> Weavers No. 2 reed.
> Handle—1 spoke No. 5 reed, 18 inches.

Weave a base over the 16 spoke center $3\frac{1}{4}$ inches. Turn up with two rows of No. 2 reed in triple twist. Hold the spokes in an outward slant and weave six rows of pairing. Draw the weavers tightly and hold the spokes in toward the center of base. Weave four rows of pairing.

Take each spoke now, pass it back of the next spoke to right, bring it down the side of the basket to the base, pass it through the two rows of triple twist.

Turn the basket upside down. Make the base stand as follows.

Working to the right, No. 1 spoke is passed in front of No. 2 spoke and back of No. 3 spoke. Each spoke is treated likewise, in front of the first to the right, and back of the second.

**HANDLE**

Insert the ends of the 18 inch spoke well down the sides of the tray. In coil effect, weave eight rows of No. 2 reed around the handle, covering it entirely, as illustrated in Model No. 18. In this tray the size should be just large enough to allow the dish to be removed easily.

## MODEL 44.—FIG. 60
### CANDY TRAY NO. 2

MATERIAL

    16 spokes No. 2 reed, 25 inches.
    Handle—2 spokes No. 5 reed, 20 inches.
    Weavers No. 2 reed.

This tray is woven similar to the preceding one, excepting the top, where the weaving is continued over the dish until five rows are finished. While weaving the last five rows, the spokes are bent in towards the dish, and the weaver pulled tight. Working in this manner holds the dish from slipping out and makes a rounded effect at the top. The handle is made of two spokes, which are pressed into an oval shape and it is finished by twisting No. 2 reed around it as shown in Fig. 60.

## MODEL 45.—FIG. 61
### CAKE TRAY

The tray is first made and then painted with white enamel.

8

MATERIAL

    8 spokes No. 5 reed, 7 inches.
    64 spokes No. 2 reed, 16 inches.
    2 spokes No. 6 reed, 26 inches.
    Weavers No. 2 reed.
    Weavers No. 3 reed.

With No. 2 reed, weave three rows around the 8 spoke center; separate the spokes with ten rows of pairing. Insert the 64 spokes. Place two each side of the base spokes. Weave two rows in triple twist with No. 3 reed, holding the No. 5 spokes with one group of twos. Now in double weaving, weave six rows, over two groups of spokes and under two groups, holding the No. 5 spoke by the side of one group of twos to the end of the base. Weave three rows No. 3 reed in triple twist, holding the spokes slightly upward while weaving. Complete with two rows of triple. First row of triple should rest on the base of basket, while the other two rows should be slightly upward on the sides. Finish with following border: Holding the under side of basket or bottom of tray toward you and weaving to right, place one group of spokes in front of next group, back of second group to the right, front of third group, back of fourth group, in front of fifth group to the right. Bring

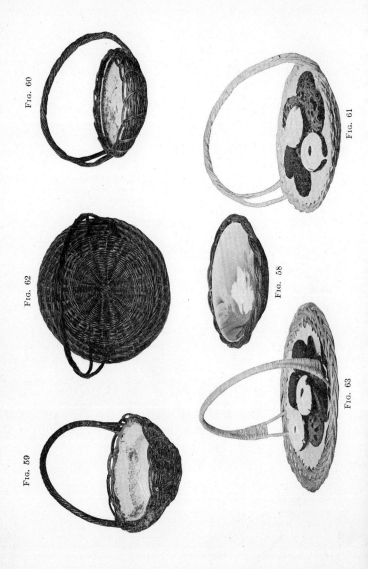

Fig. 60

Fig. 61

Fig. 62

Fig. 58

Fig. 59

Fig. 63

the spokes out to the front and down through the
two rows of triple weave.   Each group is worked
out in same manner, until all groups are facing the
weaver.

The stand for basket is woven in two rows;  first
row, each spoke is brought in front of two spokes
and in;  second row, each spoke is placed in front
of one and back of the next spoke where the ends
are cut off closely and carefully.

HANDLE

Place the ends of the spokes of handle through
the triple weaving and in back of the weaving of
base border.   Have the spokes about 2 inches
apart.   The tray is completed with a coiled handle
as shown in Fig. 61.

### MODEL 46.—FIG. 62

#### SANDWICH TRAY

This tray is worked out in the natural reed and
when completed dyed brown.

MATERIAL

       8 spokes No. 4 reed, 5 inches.
       96 spokes No. 2 reed, 20 inches.
       Weavers No. 2 reed.
       Handle—2 spokes No. 6 reed, 31 inches.

After fastening the center with two rows of weaving, weave three rows, separating the spokes in twos; then weave fourteen rows in pairing. Insert the 96 spokes, placing three spokes by the side of each spoke of No. 4 reed. After all the spokes are inserted, weave three rows of triple twist, No. 2 reed; considering each group of three spokes as one spoke, weave five rows in double weaving. With No. 2 reed, weave three rows of triple, separating the spokes in groups of twos. Complete with the following border. Consider each group of twos as one spoke. Take one group and place it over the next two groups, under the next two, over the next two, under the next two, over the next two, under the next two and out in front. Do the same with each group of spokes. Allow the first groups to be woven loosely until all the groups are woven; then draw the loose groups tight. Make the border uniform throughout. You are now ready for the border on the base of the tray. Two rows are woven to make the stand for the tray. First row, each spoke is brought in front of next three spokes and back of next three. Second row, each spoke is brought in front of the next three spokes where they are cut off inside the weaving.

HANDLE

Insert the two pieces No. 6 reed between the border and triple twist. Leave about a two inch space between the inserted spokes. Fasten securely with No. oo reed. With No. 2 weavers, weave three rows in twirl effect around one spoke, until about 4½ inches are woven up on the spokes, then considering both spokes of handle as one, continue the weaving until you are opposite to where the spokes are joined. Now coil the weaver around one spoke to the end of the handle, bringing the weaver each time down under the tray and up on the other side of spoke. Treat the other spoke in the same manner until both spokes are uniform. Hold the weaver tightly throughout the weaving of the handle. A loosely twisted coil makes a very poor handle.

If the handle is woven correctly, groups of three coils around the handle, with a space of about ¾ inch apart, will be the result.

FIG. 63

The tray is made of natural reed No. 4 and No. 2. The inner base spokes are No. 4 reed, the inserted spokes No. 2 reed. Two spokes of No. 5 reed, twenty-eight inches long, are required for the handle—the weavers, No. oo reed.

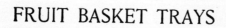

FRUIT BASKET TRAYS

# CHAPTER X
## FRUIT BASKET TRAYS

### MODEL 47.—FIG. 64
### NO. 1 FRUIT BASKET TRAY

MATERIAL

    8 spokes No. 5 reed, 8 inches.
    31 spokes No. 5 reed, 16 inches.
    1 spoke No. 8 reed, 32 inches.
    Weavers No. 2 reed.
    Weavers No. 4 reed.

Insert and fasten the spokes in position with the cross weave. Weave four rows of No. 2 reed. Follow this with twelve rows of pairing and nine rows of double weaving.

Insert the 31 spokes and weave with No. 4 reed, four rows of three-rod coil. Pinch the spokes and set up three rows of triple twist. Weave eight rows of double weaving, holding the spokes slantingly outward. Finish with three rows of triple twist and the plaited border.

HANDLE

Insert the piece of No. 8 reed down through the border, through the weaving to the lower triple twist. With No. 2 reed, coil eight rows around the handle making ten twists.

## MODEL 48.—FIG. 65
### NO. 2 FRUIT BASKET TRAY

MATERIAL

16 spokes No. 2 tan reed, 46 inches.
30 spokes No. 2 tan reed, 16 inches.
Weavers No. 2 reed.
Weavers No. 3 reed.
Tan colored dish.
Handle—2 spokes No. 5 reed, 25 inches.

Over a 16 spoke center weave a base 3½ inches, separating the spokes into groups of twos. Insert the 30 spokes. This will make groups of fours.

Turn up with two rows of No. 3 reed in triple twist. While weaving, curve the spokes to correspond to the curve of dish, draw the weavers tightly to hold the dish securely.

Follow the upset with eleven rows simple weaving. Consider every group of fours as one spoke. With two rows of triple twist in No. 3 reed, separate the groups of fours into groups of twos. Weave twenty-eight rows in simple weaving.

For the sides, take one spoke of each group, pass

it back of next two groups, bring it down the outside of basket and through the triple twist at base. The spokes will run singly on the outside of the basket, but will pass through the triple twist at the base in groups of twos. After all the groups have been passed through the triple twist the border is made as follows:

First row, each group is passed back of the next two groups to the right.

Second row, each group is passed in front of the next two groups, back of the third group where the ends are cut off closely.

## BORDER FOR TOP OF BASKET

First row, each single spoke is brought back of next two spokes.

Second row, each group is passed in front of next two groups and back of third group where the ends are cut closely.

## HANDLE

Insert the ends of handle through the weaving about 1¾ inches apart. Coil six rows around the handle and fasten ends securely.

## MODEL 49.—FIG. 66

### NO. 3 FRUIT BASKET TRAY

MATERIAL

> 8 spokes No. 5 reed, 36 inches.
> 9 spokes No. 5 reed, 15 inches.
> Weavers No. 2 reed.
> Weavers No. 3 reed.

Make a four inch base in pairing.   Turn sharply upward and slant inward with four rows of No. 3 reed in three rod twist.   Weave eight rows in No. 2 reed, over two, under one.   Change the reed to No. oo.   Weave six rows, over two spokes, under one, with three stands of No. oo reed in slewing. The weaver must constantly keep drawing the reed tight and holding the spokes well in towards the center.   With a strand of No. oo reed, make eighteen rows in the plain weave.   The diameter should be now 1¼ inches   Hold the spokes slightly outward and with three weavers in slewing, make seven rows, weaving in front of 2 spokes, back of 1 spoke.   The diameter should now be almost two inches.

Insert the 9 spokes, placing a single spoke by the side of every other spoke.   Soak all the spokes well, pinch with pliers and bend the spokes straight out-

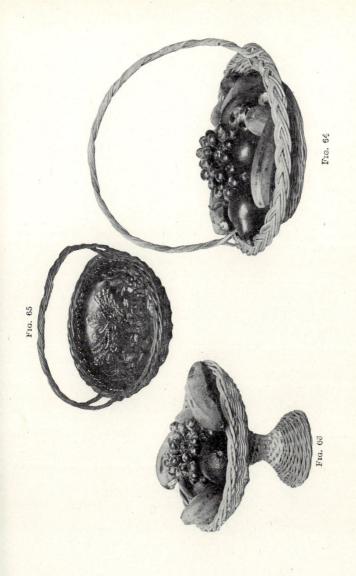

FIG. 65

FIG. 64.

FIG. 63

ward.   Hold them in this position until three rows
of pairing, three rows of triple twist No. 2 reed and
five rows of single weaving are completed.

Bend the spokes in a curved effect, hold them
slightly outward and upward.   In this position
weave ten rows double weaving.   Holding the
spokes now in a pronounced upward curve, weave
five rows of triple twist in No. 4 reed.

The following border completes the tray: Turn
down three spokes—No. 1 spoke back of No. 2,
No. 2 spoke back of No. 3, No. 3 spoke back of No.
4.   Now place No. 1 spoke in front of the third and
fourth spokes and back of the fifth spoke; likewise
place No. 2 spoke in front of the fourth and fifth
spokes and back of the sixth spoke.   Continue this
around the basket until all the spokes are woven in
the border.

## MODEL 50
### DESK TRAY

MATERIAL

> Board 12 inches by 10 inches.
> 45 spokes No. 5 reed, 19 inches.
> Weavers No. 2 reed.
> Weavers No. 4 reed.

A desk tray is a very useful article and is made
as follows:

Bore 45 holes through the board about ⅜ inch in from the edge of the board. Insert the 45 spokes through these holes allowing 3½ inches for the bottom. Make a foundation stand by weaving these end spokes in front of 2 spokes and back of the third spoke.

The sides are woven with two rows of three rod coil, then in double weaving until the tray is 2½ inches high. Follow this with two rows of triple twist and the plaited border.

### MODEL 51.—FIG. 67

#### SMALL SERVING TRAY

MATERIAL

    Board 9½ inches by 6¼ inches.
    Glass 8¾ inches by 5¾ inches.
    Cretonne 8¾ inches by 5¾ inches.
    60 spokes No. 2 reed, 15 inches.
    Weavers No. 2 reed.

Bore 60 holes through the board large enough for No. 2 reed to slip through easily. The holes should be one-half inch apart—19 holes on each of the lengthwise sides and 12 on each end.

Pass the spokes through each hole. Allow 1½ inches for the bottom of tray. For the base border weave one row of pairing and the following border: Each spoke is passed in front of the first spoke to right and back of the second spoke. When all the spokes are woven in this way, place the tray on a flat surface and make sure the base border is perfectly even and level.

The cretonne and glass should be indentical in size. Lay the cretonne on the board flat and even, and place the glass over it. The glass must fit snugly and tightly to make a perfect tray. Keep the spokes moist to allow easy weaving. The weavers must be soaked until very pliable. Weave ½ inch of pairing with No. 2 reed or nine rows. Follow this with one row of triple twist in No. 3 reed. The plaited border completes the tray.

A very pretty effect may be obtained by having a pale pink flowered cretonne and natural color reed. The cretonne and color of reed should always harmonize.

## MODEL 52

### OBLONG SERVING TRAY

MATERIAL

Board 17 inches by 12 inches.
Cretonne 16¼ inches by 11½ inches.
Glass 16¼ inches by 11½ inches.
99 spokes No. 5 brown reed, 19 inches.
Weavers No. 4 reed.
Brown stain.

Bore 99 holes through board equal distance apart. Stain the board brown. Insert the spokes and allow 3½ inches for the bottom stand. Make a border for this stand in the following manner:

First row, each spoke is brought back of next spoke to right.

Second row, each spoke is passed in front of the next spoke and in back of the next where the end is cut off.

The sides are now woven. A 4-rod coil No. 4 reed holds the glass firmly in place. Follow this with seven rows double weaving No. 2 brown reed and one row No. 4 reed in 4-rod coil. Complete the tray with the plaited border.

After the tray is finished, singe it to get rid of all the loose bits of reed—then polish the board with two or three coats of wax. The cretonne, reed and stain should harmonize in color. A soft brush produces best results in polishing the basket.

## MODEL 53

### OVAL SERVING TRAY

MATERIAL

       Board 20 inches by 14 inches.
       Glass 19 inches by 13 inches.
       Cretonne 19 inches by 13 inches.
       52 spokes No. 5 brown reed, 20 inches.
       Weavers No. 4 reed.

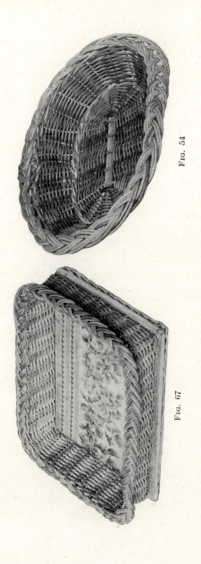

FIG. 54

FIG. 67

The holes should be made about one inch apart. Insert the 52 spokes and make foundation stand as described under preceding model. Be careful that the board is perfectly dry before placing the cretonne upon it. Keep the spokes moist by using a wet sponge; be careful not to allow any water to get under the glass while weaving. Best results are obtained by staining the board first and then weaving a dyed reed; good results, however, may be obtained by making the tray in natural reed first and then staining the board and reed. Great care must be exercised in painting the tray after it is made.

The sides of the oval tray are woven two inches high. First weave one row of 4-rod coil then seven rows of double weaving in pairing. One row of 4-rod coil and the plaited border completes the tray. Polish as described under preceding model.

## MODEL 54
### ROUND SERVING TRAY

MATERIAL

Diameter of board 10 inches.
Diameter of glass 9¼ inches.
Diameter of cretonne 9¼ inches.
39 spokes No. 4 reed, 20 inches.
Weavers No. 4 reed.

9

Prepare the board by making 39 holes ⅝ of an inch from edge of board, ¾ inch spacing between each hole. Insert the 39 spokes. Weave an under base stand in the following manner: First row, each spoke is brought back of next spoke to right and out in front. Second row, each spoke is passed in front of next spoke to right and in back of second spoke where it is cut off.

This base weaving should be uniform throughout so that the tray base may be perfectly even. Stand the tray on a flat desk and see that each spoke touches the desk. For the side of the tray weave one row of 4-rod wale and finish the ends in the usual way.

Insert one No. 4 weaver and weave nine rows around the tray. Introduce four weavers and work one row of 4-rod coil. Finish the tray with the plaited border.

# SCRAP BASKETS

# CHAPTER XI

## SCRAP BASKETS

### MODEL 55.—FIG 68.

#### SMALL SCRAP BASKET (CHECKER DESIGN)

MATERIAL

    8 spokes No. 4 reed, 6 inches.
    31 spokes No. 4 reed, 19 inches.
    Weavers No. 2 reed.
    Weavers No. 4 reed.
    Handle—2 spokes No. 6 reed, 10 inches.

Weave a base 5¾ inches. Insert 31 spokes and weave the sides 8½ inches high, in the following manner:

Turn the spokes up with two rows of triple twist No. 4 reed, then six rows of double weaving in No. 2 reed. Change to blue No. 4 reed and make a coil of triple twist; then in blue and white check weave sixteen rows. Follow this with one row of No. 4 blue reed in triple twist. Change the reed to No. 2 natural and weave twelve rows in double weaving. One row of blue No. 4 reed, triple twist, follows this, then sixteen rows of blue and white check

(2 checks) and one row of blue No. 4 reed in triple. Change the reed again and work five rows double weaving in No. 2 reed. Follow this with two rows of triple twist and the border described under Model 22.

Insert the ends of the handle well down amid the weaving and with No. 2 reed make four coils around the handle.

### MODEL 56.—FIG. 69

#### LARGE SCRAP BASKET (CHECKER DESIGN)

##### MATERIAL

      8 spokes No. 5 reed, 8 inches.
      31 spokes No. 5 reed, 27 inches.
      Weavers No. 4 blue reed.
      Weavers No. 4 natural reed.

Weave a base 7½ inches. Insert 31 spokes and turn up with four rows of triple. Weave twelve rows single weaving in No. 4 natural reed, then one row in triple twist, No. 4 blue reed. Seven checks in blue and natural follow this. Weave one row in triple with No. 4 blue reed and twelve rows No. 4 natural.

Follow this with three rows of triple in No. 4 natural reed.

FIG. 68

FIG. 69

Complete the basket with plaited border described under Model 14.

## MODEL 57.—FIG. 70
### SCRAP BASKET IN OVAL REED

MATERIAL

      8 spokes No. 5 reed, 6½ inches.
      31 spokes No. 5 reed, 27 inches.
      Weavers No. 4 reed.
      Weavers No. 5 oval reed.
      Handle—2 spokes No. 6 reed, 46 inches.

Weave a base 6 inches. Insert 31 spokes. Pinch sharply and turn up with three rows of triple No. 5 reed. In No. 5 oval reed make forty-six rows, placing the weaver over 3 spokes and back of 2 spokes. Carry this weave throughout the basket. Finish with three rows of triple in No. 5 reed and the plaited border.

HANDLE

Make two rings for the ring handles and fasten them to the sides of the basket.

## MODEL 58.—FIG. 71

### RUSH SCRAP BASKET

MATERIAL

    8 spokes No. 5 reed, 8 inches.
    31 spokes No. 5 reed, 27 inches.
    Weavers No. 5 reed.
    Weavers braided rush.

Over an 8 spoke foundation, weave a base 7½ inches in pairing, with No. 4 reed.

Insert 31 spokes No. 5 reed. Pinch sharply and turn the spokes upward with three rows triple twist in No. 5 reed. In single weaving, weave twenty rows of braided rush. Complete the sides with four rows of triple twist in No. 5 reed. The plaited border completes the basket.

While weaving, the spokes should be held slantingly outward. Care should be exercised not to spread the spokes outward too much as this will spoil the shape of basket. The diameter at the top of the basket, when finished, should be twelve inches.

## MODEL 59

### NO. 2 FLOWER BASKET

MATERIAL

8 spokes No. 4 reed, 4½ inches.
26 spokes No. 4 reed, 18 inches.
11 spokes No. 4 reed, 12 inches.
Weavers No. 2 reed.
Weavers No. 3 reed.
Weavers No. 4 reed.
Handle—1 spoke No. 8 reed, 30 inches.

Weave a base in pairing, 3¾ inches. Turn sharply upward with three rows of triple weave. Hold the spokes straight and weave, with No. 2 reed, three inches in pairing. Take a strand of No. 3 reed and weave six rows. Begin the shaping of the basket by holding the side spokes upright and bend the end spokes sharply down the outside of the basket. Continue the weaving until sixteen more rows are woven.

Insert the 11 spokes, between the end spokes of the basket—5 spokes on one end and 6 on the other.

Weave eight rows of triple twist and the border described under Model 22.

Insert the handle spoke, down the side of the basket. In the coil twist, weave five rows. Fasten the ends of the weavers securely.

## MODEL 60

### NO. 3 FLOWER BASKET

MATERIAL

    6½ spokes No. 5 reed, 6 inches.

    26 spokes No. 5 reed, 24 inches.

    15 spokes No. 5 reed, 12 inches.

    Weavers No. 2 reed.

    Weavers No. 4 reed.

    Handle—1 spoke No. 8 reed, 20 inches.

Complete a base five inches. Insert 26 spokes and turn sharply with three rows of triple weave. Hold the spoke straight upward, and make seventeen rows No. 2 reed, weaving over two spokes and under one spoke. Introduce slew wale with two weavers. Work twelve rows, over two spokes under one spoke.

Insert the 15 spokes, 8 at one end and 7 at the other end. Weave two rows of 3-rod coil. Wet the spokes well and bend the end spokes down the outside of the basket. Hold the spokes in this position during the rest of the weaving—that is, hold the side spokes erect and the end spokes in a downward flare. Introduce two No. 2 weavers and make fifteen rows in pairing. Open the end spokes and bend them down. Weave seven rows in triple twist with No. 4 reed. Finish with the border described under Model 22.

Insert the 20 inch spoke for handle. Weave, in coil effect, four rows around the handle. Fasten the handle securely to the basket.

UTILITY BASKETS

# CHAPTER XII
## UTILITY BASKETS

### MODEL 61.—FIG. 72
### ARTISTIC BASKET WITH LID

MATERIAL

    10 spokes No. 5 reed, 6 inches.
    21 spokes No. 5 reed, 18 inches.
    Weavers No. 4 reed.
    Weavers No. 2 reed.
    Lid—16 spokes No. 4 reed, 15 inches.

Make a bottom in the ordinary way, 5½ inches. Insert the spokes, pinch, and make an upsetting four rows in 3-rod coil. Hold the spokes in a slightly slanting outward direction during the weaving of the basket. In plain weave, make 2¼ inches. Follow this with four rows triple weave and the border described under Model 22.

LID

Arrange the spokes in position. In ribbon weave, work one row No. ∞ reed. With No. 1 reed, weave four rows in pairing. Hold the spokes to secure a curved center for lid. Separate the spokes into groups of twos with five rows of pairing. Separate into single spokes with two rows triple twist No. 2 reed. Holding the spokes in an outward position, weave nine rows pairing. Wet the spokes and place the lid on a flat board or table. Press the spokes flat on the board and weave two rows of No. 4 reed in triple twist. In plain weave, work six rows. Complete the weaving with the following border: Turn the lid upside down. Take each spoke back of next spoke to the right, bring it to the front of the lid. Second row, each spoke is passed in front of next two spokes and back of the third spoke, where it is cut off.

## HANDLE

Make a ring $1\frac{1}{4}$ inches in diameter. Fasten it to the center of the lid by weaving the ends in and out amid the weaving of lid.

## FIG. 73

The base spokes of this "Knitting Basket" are of No. 4 reed. The inserted spokes are of No. 3 reed, twenty-two inches long. The weavers are of No. 2 and No. 3 reed.

FIG. 72

FIG. 73

FIG. 71

FIG. 70

## MODEL 62.—FIG. 74

### MOTHER'S SEWING BASKET

MATERIAL

 8 spokes No. 5 reed, 7 inches.
 62 spokes No. 4 reed, 18 inches.
 Weavers—No. 4 reed.

Weave a base seven inches in pairing. Insert the spokes, pinch, and turn with an upsetting of four rows 3-rod coil. Bend and hold the spokes outward. Work four inches in plain weave No. 4 reed. Wet the spokes, pinch and bend inward. Weave two inches plain weave. Make four rows triple twist. Complete the basket with the following border: First row, each group of spokes is brought back of the next group to the right and passed out to the front. Second row, each group is passed over the next four groups, back of the fifth group where it is cut off.

## MODEL 63.—FIG. 75

### LILY BASKET

MATERIAL

 8 spokes No. 5 reed, 6½ inches.
 62 spokes No. 4 reed, 18 inches.
 Weavers No. 2 reed.
 Weavers No. 4 reed.

 10

With No. 1 reed, fasten the spokes with three rows of pairing. Separate into groups of twos, with two rows of pairing. Separate into single groups, with two rows of pairing. Insert two No. 4 weavers and work ten rows in pairing. This makes a 6½ inch base.

Insert the spokes, two spokes each side of the base spokes. Turn up with an upsetting of four rows of triple twist No. 4 reed. The spokes are double and carried double throughout the basket. Hold the spokes so that the basket will slant outward. Weave four inches in plain weave. Wet the spokes and pinch sharply. Bend the spokes inward. Work one row in 3-rod coil. Follow this with fifteen rows in plain weave. Bending the spokes slightly upward, work five rows in triple weave. Cut off one spoke of each group. Complete the basket with the border described under Model 22.

## MODEL 64.—FIG. 76

### SMALL BARREL SHAPED RUSH BASKET

MATERIAL

         8 spokes No. 5 reed, 6½ inches.
         31 spokes No. 5 reed, 20 inches.
         Weavers No. 4 reed.
         Weavers No. 5 reed.
         Weavers braided rush.

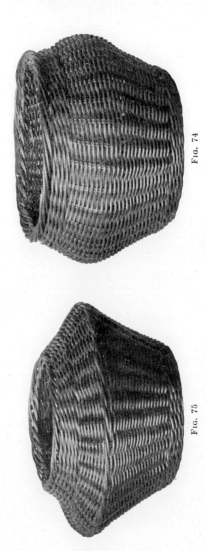

Fig. 74

Fig. 75

Make a round bottom six inches in diameter. Insert the 31 spokes and make an upsetting of six rows of 3-rod wale No. 5 reed. Throughout the basket, hold the spokes equal distance apart; weave carefully and evenly.

Prepare the rush for weaving by soaking it in water until it is moist, or wet enough to keep it from cracking. Do not try to weave the braided rush dry as it cracks easily. Slant the spokes outward, introduce the rush and weave eight rows of simple weaving. Wet the spokes well and bend them in. Have the rush moistened and weave six rows, drawing the spokes in, to secure the rounded effect. Introduce three weavers of No. 4 reed, and work five rows of 3-rod wale. Complete the basket with the following border:

First row, each spoke is carried back of the next two spokes to the right and out to the front. Second row, each spoke is passed in front of the next two spokes to the right, and back of the third where it is cut off.

## MODEL 65.—FIG. 77

### LARGE RUSH SCRAP BASKET

MATERIAL

    8 spokes No. 6 reed, 7½ inches.
    62 spokes No. 5 reed, 31 inches.
    Weavers No. 4 reed.
    Weavers No. 5 reed.

Make a round base seven inches in diameter. Insert the 62 spokes, placing two spokes each side of the base spokes. Weave two rows of triple twist. Turn the spokes sharply upward, weave four rows of triple weave and eight rows of plain weave. Insert three weavers and work two rows of triple.

Soak the rush a few minutes in cold water and with it work fourteen rows in single weaving. Where any ends of rush are joined sew them carefully with fine raffia.

Insert three weavers and make seven rows in triple twist. Throughout the basket each set of 2 spokes is treated as 1 spoke.

Do not cut any of the spokes off. Make a plaited border with the double spokes. The spokes should be held slantingly outward, while weaving, to obtain the desired shape.

FIG. 76

FIG. 77

## MODEL 66

### OBLONG TRAY

This tray will not only be of use on the dressing table, but will add to its beauty and daintiness; it also serves for an ideal comb and brush tray. Dimensions 9½ inches by 6¼ inches.

MATERIAL

> 9 spokes No. 4 reed, 15 inches.
> 13 spokes No. 4 reed, 15 inches.
> Weavers No. 2 reed.
> Weavers No. 3 reed.

Place the 9 spokes in a horizontal position, equal distances apart; or if two pieces of wood, nine inches long, are available, make 9 holes in each piece ¾ inch apart. Through these holes insert the nine 15 inch spokes. This holds the spokes in a firm position and makes the weaving simpler.

Take two pieces of the 15 inch spokes and weave as 1 spoke, one row in simple weaving. Now insert a strand of No. 2 reed and make eleven rows simple weaving, working the first row under and over the same spokes as the two 15 inch spokes are woven.

Weave one 15 inch spoke, weaving from right to left, under the first spoke and over the second. Introduce a No. 2 weaver, and work eleven rows, beginning under the first spoke and over the second. Weave another No. 4 spoke.   Continue in this way, first one No. 4 spoke, and then ten or eleven rows of No. 2 reed, until the thirteen pieces of No. 4 reed are woven.   Both ends of the tray should have two No. 4 spokes woven as one.   The weaving should now measure 9 inches by 6 inches.

Weave one row of triple twist around the tray. Wet and turn both end and side spokes sharply upward.   Make an upset of three rows of triple.

With the spokes moist, weave the following border:

First row, each spoke is brought back of the next spoke to the right and out to the front.

Second row, each spoke is passed in front of next three spokes to the right and back of the fourth where it is cut off.

## MODEL 67

### UTILITY BASKET

**Material**

        8 spokes No. 5 reed, 6½ inches.
        31 spokes No. 5 reed, 22 inches.
        Weavers No. 2 reed.
        Weavers No. 4 reed.

Work a base 6½ inches in the usual way.   Insert

the 31 spokes and make an upset of three rows of triple twist. Work nine rows of double weaving No. 2 reed. Introduce three weavers and make two rows of triple. With No. 2 reed, work nine rows more in double weaving. Follow this with two rows of No. 4 reed in triple, twelve rows double, three rows triple, twelve rows pairing No. 4 reed and seven rows No. 4 reed in 4-rod coil.

Complete the basket with the border described under Model 22.

The basket is enameled in white and gold and makes a very pretty effect. The base border and the top of the base are painted in gold.

## MODEL 68.—FIG. 78
### SCRAP BASKET (OPEN WORK)

MATERIAL

    8 spokes No. 5 reed, 9 inches.
    31 spokes No. 5 reed, 29 inches.
    31 spokes No. 5 reed, 15 inches.
    Weavers No. 4 reed.
    Weavers No. 5 reed.

Make a base 8½ inches in double weaving No. 4 reed. Insert the 31 29-inch spokes. Turn sharply upward and make one row of 3-rod coil. Insert the 31 15-inch spokes and work three rows of triple twist. The spokes are now double and should be held straight. Make eight rows double weaving and four rows in triple. Leave one inch space open. Find the middle of a long weaver, place it around one of the double spokes and weave seven rows in pairing.

Now separate the double spokes into single spokes with two rows triple twist. Leave another inch of open space in the basket. Take the middle of another weaver and, holding the spokes double again, weave four rows in pairing.

Leave an open space of two inches. Weave three rows of pairing. Number the groups 1, 2, 3, 4, 5.

Hold the second spoke of No. 1 group straight. Cross the first spoke of No. 3 group over the second spoke of No. 2 group, and place it by the side of No. 1 group, where it is held in this position by placing the middle of a weaver around it, and drawing one end of the weaver to the inside of the basket, the other end to the outside of basket. Hold the second spoke of No. 2 group straight, cross the first spoke of No. 4 group over the second spoke of No. 3 group and place it by the side of the second spoke of No. 2 group. This is held in po-

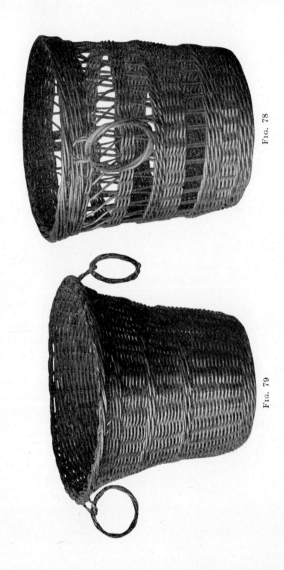

Fig. 78

Fig. 79

sition by another twist of pairing. Take the first spoke of No. 5 group, cross it over second spoke of No. 4 group, and place it in position by the side of second spoke of No. 3 group, where it is held in position by a twist of pairing. Weave one row of pairing around the basket holding the spokes in this position. The second spoke of each group is held straight, while the first spoke of the third group to the right is crossed over the second group and placed by the side of the first group, where it is held in position by pairing. Two more rows of pairing are woven holding the double spokes side by side. Follow this with three rows of 4-rod coil.

The basket is finished with border described under Model 22.

Make ring handles and place in position on opposite sides of basket.

## MODEL 69.—FIG. 79

### FANCY SCRAP BASKET

MATERIAL

    8 spokes No. 5 reed, 7½ inches.
    62 spokes No. 4 reed, 27 inches.
    Weavers No. 4 reed.

Work a base 6½ inches. Insert the spokes and make an upset of four rows 3-rod coil. The basket is worked with double side spokes. Hold the spokes straight and weave twenty-nine rows in plain weave. Bend the spokes slightly outward. Weave two rows 3-rod coil, seventeen rows single, two rows 3-rod coil, sixteen rows single and five rows triple twist.

The plaited border completes the weaving of the basket.

Make ring handles and fasten on opposite sides of basket.


## MODEL 70.—FIG. 80

### ARTISTIC SCRAP BASKET

This basket is first made, then enameled in white with suggestions of gold.

MATERIAL

      8 spokes No. 5 reed, 7½ inches.
      33 spokes No. 5 reed, 29 inches.
      Weavers No. 4 reed.
      Weavers No. 5 reed.

In the ordinary way work a round base seven inches in diameter. Insert the 33 spokes. Make an upset of four rows 3-rod coil. Weave ten rows plain weave, eight rows double, and twelve rows pairing. Introduce three weavers and work three

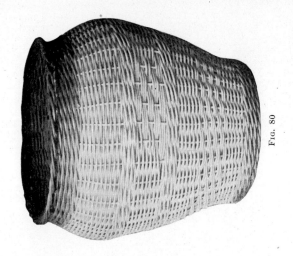

Fig. 80

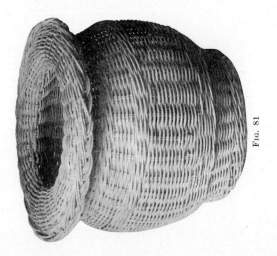

Fig. 81

rows 3-rod coil. The following design is worked in the basket on opposite sides: Number the spokes 1 to 33. The design is inserted between the spokes Nos. 11 to 17 (eleven to seventeen) inclusive, and between the spokes Nos. 27 to 33 (twenty-seven to thirty-three) inclusive. Insert a weaver back of any spoke, which may be called No. 1 spoke, and work one row around the basket in plain weave. In the second and third rows, between the spokes Nos. 11 to 17 (eleven to seventeen) and Nos. 27 to 33 (twenty-seven to thirty-three) the weaver should pass back and in front of the same spokes as in No. 1 row. That is, in the first three rows the weaver should pass back of Nos. 11, 13, 15, 17 spokes, in front of Nos. 12, 14, 16 spokes, back of Nos. 27, 29, 31, 33 spokes, in front of Nos. 28, 30, 32 spokes. In the fourth, fifth and sixth rows the weaver passes back of Nos. 12, 14, 16 spokes, front of Nos. 13, 15 spokes, back of Nos. 28, 30, 32 spokes, in front of Nos. 29, 31 spokes. In the seventh, eighth and ninth rows the weaver passes back of Nos. 13, 15 spokes, in front of No. 14 spoke, back of Nos. 29, 31 spokes, in front of No. 30 spoke. The tenth, eleventh and twelfth rows of weaving pass over and under the same spokes as the fourth, fifth and sixth rows. Likewise the

thirteenth, fourteenth and fifteenth rows correspond to first, second and third rows, which complete the design.

Between Nos. 1 to 10 spokes and Nos. 18 to 26
spokes, the weaving is the simple over and under
weave. Owing to insertion of design it is sometimes necessary to pass the weaver back of two
spokes to get the correct weave. Follow the
fifteen rows of weaving with three rows of triple
twist. Bend the spokes inward while making the
triple twist. Holding the spokes in the same
position work twenty rows plain weave. Follow
this with five rows triple twist. Complete the
basket with the border under Model 14.

### MODEL 71.—FIG. 81

#### FATHER'S WASTE PAPER BASKET

MATERIAL

 8 spokes No. 5 reed, 8 inches.
 31 spokes No. 5 reed, 28 inches.
 Weavers No. 4 reed.
 Weavers No. 5 reed.

Make a seven inch base No. 4 reed. Insert the
31 spokes and turn up with five rows of upsetting
No. 5 reed. Weave fifteen rows single weaving.

Insert four weavers and work four rows, each weaver passing in front of three spokes and back of one spoke. From the beginning hold the spokes outward. In plain weave, work twenty-six rows. Wet the spokes well now and bend them in. Introduce three weavers and work three rows of triple twist. Drop two weavers and work eleven rows in plain weaving. The weaver should be drawn tightly from now on. Weave two rows in 3-rod coil. Drop two weavers and work sixteen rows in plain weaving. Wet the spokes again and with the plier press the spokes well and bend them outward for a slight flare. Work seventeen rows in plain weave. Bend the spokes down and make three rows of triple twist No. 5 reed. Finish with the following border:

First row, place each spoke back of the next spoke to the right.

Second row, carry each spoke over the next 3 spokes and down to the outside of basket where it rests under the fourth spoke. Cut off the ends sharply.

# A FEW WORDS ON DYEING

## CHAPTER XIII
## A FEW WORDS ON DYEING

The art of dyeing has been of interest to the peoples of all nations and in all ages. History shows us that just so soon as man's covering or clothing, the furs and skins of animals, was discarded for wool, linen or cotton materials, just so soon was the desire or want for colors made manifest. Man began the study of coloring, of staining and dyeing; he experimented, and in his new need he worked to reproduce the reds, the purples, the blues and the yellows of nature's exquisite canvas, with what success and failure we have a fair knowledge.

Nothing appeared too small or too unimportant to put in use in order to gain the desired results. Vegetables, fruits, plants, barks of trees and sometimes ludicrous mixtures were part of the workings for this purpose, all of which did meet with rewards —for dyes and beautiful colors were discovered.

From the plant *indigoferae* was obtained a blue stain, known as indigo. Specimens of dyeing found in the Egyptian tombs show examples of indigo dye. This plant (*indigoferae*) grows and is industriously and profitably cultivated in South America and India. It was imported by the Romans from India, getting its name from that country. Two other important dyestuffs discovered in the early ages were saffron, which gives yellow shades, and madder-root, or to be more specific, the roots of madder, which produces brown and purple shades.

Thus was obtained and supplied the blue dye from vegetable or plant life; and from animal life came the most beautiful red dyes.

Cochineal, lac and kermes better known as "grain colors" and called so because of their general resemblance to grain, are really the dried bodies of insects, minute in size, called "cocci" berries, which lived and thrived on certain kinds of bushes and trees and which, after months of care, were taken from their berths and dried.

These dyestuffs, used of course with a mordant, produce beautiful shades, which are fast to water and light.

Perhaps no greater nor more remarkable changes have been made in any industry than in that of dyeing, for, the saving of labor, energy, time and money by the use of modern chemical agencies is of a magnitude not easily appreciable. New ways have completely supplanted the old. This revolution was due to the accidental discovery of mauveine by Sir William Henry Perkin, who by this and his later experiments enriched the world with one of its most important discoveries. After his discoveries became known great factories sprang up throughout Europe manufacturing coal-tar dyestuffs, shortly producing the "Basic dyes." Perkin's discovery served as a stimulus to other chemists, who, working unceasingly, soon produced quantities of dyestuffs, which are designated as "Aniline Colors."

Though progress has been made and the discoveries have simplified greatly the processes of dyeing, this does not mean that experimenting has ceased. By no means. Today interested and enthusiastic workers are anxiously and patiently experimenting, and hoping to find something new; perhaps they will, or it may be you, who, through your experimenting, will uncover to the world a new wonderful dyestuff.

In preparing raffia for work, take care to shake it well. You will find that the best and easiest way to make it take the dye will be to soak it over night. If this is not practicable then soak it at

least three hours. Dissolve the dye in vinegar—
the dye bath should be warm.

The "Basic Colors" will give satisfaction, but I
would suggest in cases where a great deal of work
is to be done that the fast acid colors be used.

The color work in basketry plays a very important part as well as a fascinating one. There are
numerous ways in which a basket or tray may be
touched up, giving a charm to it that is most pleasing to the eye and attractive to the craftsman.

The entire basket may be made first, and then
either dipped, allowed to stand in the dye a few
minutes, or boiled five to thirty minutes; it may
be painted with Easy dye, stained with any desirable furniture stain, varnished and waxed up. The
basket may be finished off by using either fine sand-
paper, or powdered pumice stone, but in finishing
colored baskets, it will be found that singeing will
be the most successful method.

Again to have a contrasting color with the
natural or two tints of the same color, the reed
should be dyed first and then the desired effect
worked out.

In dyeing reed allow it to soak in a mordant for
two hours. This opens the pores and makes the
dye a permanent part of the basket. Three ounces

of alum to one quart of water makes a good mordant for many vegetable dyes.

Beautiful shades of brown, green, blue and red may be obtained by using logwood, indigo, fustic, cutch, madder, cochineal, and copperas. A very pleasing finish is secured by painting or staining the article with Light Oil Finish, combining it with turpentine in whatever proportion desired. Malachite green stain used with turpentine and Light Oil Finish make a very attractive pale green. The alert basket maker, who desires to experiment, must be on the watch in the autumn for natural dyeing material. The leaves and flowers of plants, the bark of trees, berries, etc., may be used most successfully in obtaining very desirable dye, and with patience and care beautiful and delicate shades may be obtained from vegetable dyes.

The following recipes may be used for vegetable dyeing:

## Brown

Dissolve two teaspoonfuls of madder in one quart of water. Allow the reed to soak in it five hours.

## Yellow Brown No. 1

Soak the reed for several hours in logwood

extract—obtained by boiling logwood chips in water twenty minutes.

## Yellow Brown No. 2

Mix in a quart of water two tablespoonfuls of cutch extract, adding one and a half tablespoonfuls of fustic. Boil the reed in this solution for two hours, but test.

## Olive Brown No. 1

Dissolve two tablespoonfuls of cutch, two table-spoonfuls of fustic, and one-half spoonful of log-wood in a quart of water. Boil the reed two hours in this composition.

## Olive Brown No. 2

Boil the material several hours in a composition of one and one-half pounds of walnut bark, five teaspoonfuls of washing soda and one-half cup of rock alum.

## Yellow No. 1

A good yellow can be obtained by experimenting with smartweed.

## Yellow No. 2

Mordant the reed in a solution of alum, and boil it in an extract of fustic, a half hour.

## Green

Mordant the reed in a solution of alum and water, and then dye it in the solution composition —three teaspoonfuls of indigo, a small crystal of copperas, and three pints of water. After the material is removed and washed dip it in a solution of bark extract and water.

## Olive Green

Mordant the reed in a solution of two teaspoonfuls of copperas in one quart of water. Boil the reed then in the following solution: To three teaspoonfuls of bark extract in a quart of water, add a half teaspoonful of indigo and a small quantity of logwood.

## Indian Red

Dissolve in about a quart of boiling water two tablespoonfuls of cutch extract and a small crystal of blue-stone. Boil the material in this solution until the desired color is obtained.